200

FAMILY SLOW COOKER RECIPES

HAMLYN **ALL COLOR COOKBOOK**

200
FAMILY SLOW
COOKER RECIPES

S A R A   L E W I S

An Hachette UK Company
www.hachette.co.uk

First published in Great Britain in 2016 by
Hamlyn, a division of Octopus Publishing Group Ltd.
Carmelite House, 50 Victoria Embankment,
London EC4Y 0DZ
www.octopusbooks.co.uk

Some of this material previously appeared in other books
published by Hamlyn.

Distributed in the US by Hachette Book Group, 1290 Avenue
of the Americas, 4th and 5th Floors, New York, NY 10020

Distributed in Canada by Canadian Manda Group,
664 Annette St., Toronto, Ontario, Canada M6S 2C8

ISBN 978-0-600-63218-4

Printed and bound in China.

10 9 8 7 6 5 4 3 2 1

Eggs should be medium unless otherwise stated. This book
contains dishes made with raw or lightly cooked eggs. It is
prudent for more vulnerable people such as pregnant and
nursing mothers, invalids, the elderly, babies, and young
children to avoid uncooked or lightly cooked dishes made
with eggs. Once prepared these dishes should be kept
refrigerated and used promptly.

Ovens should be preheated to the specific temperature.
If using a convection oven, follow the manufacturer's
instructions for adjusting the time and the temperature.

This book includes dishes made with nuts and nut
derivatives. It is advisable for customers with known allergic
reactions to nuts and nut derivatives and those who may be
potentially vulnerable to these allergies, such as pregnant
and nursing mothers, invalids, the elderly, babies, and
children, to avoid dishes made with nuts and nut oils. It is
also prudent to check the labels of pre-prepared ingredients
for the possible inclusion of nut derivatives.

Although cooking on low is completely safe, if you're home
during the process, the U.S. Department of Agriculture
recommends cooking on high for an hour first to ensure the
food is thoroughly cooked.

contents

introduction

introduction

Slow cooking is fashionable again and what easier way is there to make a meal than in a slow cooker? It's less expensive than turning on the oven, since it uses much less electricity, and a slow cooker is compact, too.

The food cooks gradually and gently, so vegetables become wonderfully flavorful and meat becomes meltingly tender, which means that cheaper cuts of meat can be given the five-star treatment in a slow cooker. Buy food items in bulk and make double quantities, so you can freeze half for another meal. Or, make smaller amounts of meat go further by combining them with healthy root and Mediterranean vegetables, legumes, grains, and lentils.

But a slow cooker isn't just for casseroles and stews, great though they are. You can make a huge variety of other dishes with this gadget, including lighter meals, delicious fish recipes, and child-pleasing suppers. Try warming main-meal soups, such as Pumpkin, Carrot & Quinoa (see page 22) or Country Mushroom & Bacon (see page 38); kids' favorites, such as Baked Tuna and Pasta (see page 48) and Chicken & Mango Curry (see page 54); everyday favorites, such as White Beans with Chipotle Chile (see page 80), and Piri Piri Chicken (see page 92); easy shortcuts, such as Red Bell Pepper & Chorizo Tortilla (see page 120) and Thai Beef Curry (see page 138), and food to impress, such as Seafood Laksa (see page 150) and Rioja-braised Lamb with Olives (see page 170). To finish things off, nostalgic desserts like Sticky Toffee Pudding (see page 188) and Plum & Blueberry Betty (see page 186) can become home-cooked treats once more with a slow cooker.

If you're unfamiliar with using a slow cooker, the redistribution of time involved may seem odd. Early on in the day, you spend 15 minutes in the kitchen doing a little prep, and add everything to the slow cooker. Then, you can walk away and get on with something else. While cooking before you rush out to work in the morning may not be for everyone, getting a lovely supper into the slow cooker before you head out to the golf course, for a day of shopping with a friend, or before playing taxi driver to and from the kids' clubs, may seem more manageable.

The slow cooker cooks so gently there's no need to stir or check on the food because there is no danger of it drying out or spoiling. Just enjoy the welcoming aroma of a delicious supper ready and waiting when you walk back in through the door.

New to slow cooking? Your questions answered

Are all slow cookers the same?

All slow cookers cook food slowly, though they do vary slightly. Oval-shaped slow cookers offer the most flexibility when it comes to cooking bone-in roasts or desserts. Generally, slow cookers come in three sizes:

- a two-portion size with a capacity of 3½ quarts
- a four-portion size with a capacity of 4 quarts
- a six-to-eight portion size with a capacity of 6 quarts.

Newer models might come with cooking pots that can be used on the stove, so you can fry meat or onions prior to slow cooking them in the slow-cooker pot itself. This reduces dishwashing, but these types tend to cost more. A good nonstick skillet used in conjunction with a slow cooker works just as well.

As with all things, price varies considerably. The larger models are often sold at a reduced price, but unless your family is large or you plan to cook double quantities in order to freeze half of the batch, you may find that, while the machine itself is a good price, you have to cook larger quantities than you had expected in order to just half-fill it.

When selecting a slow cooker, choose a machine with a high and low setting and an on/off light at the front of the machine so that you can easily see when it is cooking. There is nothing more frustrating than to come back eight hours later, expecting a hot, delicious meal, only to find that you haven't turned the machine on! Some models have a setting that allows you to keep the food warm, which is useful. Digital-clock features are great, but they are certainly not essential.

It may seem like a chore but, once you've purchased a slow cooker, make sure you read the handbook. The majority of models should *not* be preheated with an empty slow-cooker pot. If you part-prep the food the night before and put the earthenware slow-cooker pot in the refrigerator, all manufacturers agree that you should let it stand at room temperature for 20 minutes before adding it to the slow-cooker machine and turning it on.

Is it safe to leave it on all day?

Yes—the slow cooker runs on such a small amount of power (the equivalent of two lightbulbs) that it is safe to leave it on all day, even if you go out. Because the heat is so low and the lid forms a seal, there is no danger of the food boiling dry. The sides of the slow cooker will feel warm to the touch, so make sure you leave the machine on an uncluttered part of your kitchen countertop.

Do I have to fry foods before I add them to the slow-cooker pot?

Foods will not brown in a slow cooker, so frying onions and browning meat adds color and flavor to the finished dish. It isn't essential, however, and it's very much a matter of personal taste. The idea of frying foods before you rush out in the morning may not fill you with enthusiasm, especially if are dressed for work, so there are plenty of recipes in the book that can be made without precooking. Boosting the color and flavor with tomato paste, red wine or beer, spices, or herbs will do the trick. But if you have a young family, it can be great to come back from dropping the children off at school and get supper going in the slow cooker while things are quieter.

Does liquid have to be hot before going in the slow cooker?

The slow cooker works by building up heat to just below boiling point, then safely maintaining the heat so that food cooks gently but without any danger of allowing the bacteria that cause food poisoning to proliferate. If you add all cold ingredients, this will obviously extend the heating-up process, so add 2 to 3 hours to the cooking time, with the first hour on high, especially if the recipe states to use hot stock. But it is much quicker and very simple to dissolve a stock cube in boiling water and add the hot stock to the slow-cooker pot. And always add hot liquid when cooking a large roast.

How full should the pot be?

Ideally, the slow-cooker pot should be half full and up to three-quarters full for it to work efficiently. For soups, fill it so that the liquid is 2 inches from the top. If you have a very large slow cooker, prepare quantities to serve six to eight people, then freeze the extra in single portions or portion sizes that will suit your family to use on another occasion. As the slow cooker heats up, the steam generated will condense and make a water seal between the lid and top of the slow-cooker pot—this is perfectly normal.

Can I use my ordinary recipes?

Yes, of course. Stews, casseroles, and pot-roast recipes can all be made in the slow cooker using the same ingredients. The slow cooker creates a seal during cooking, however, so the liquid doesn't evaporate. This means you'll need to reduce the liquid in your recipes by one-third, and sometimes even by half. For stews or casseroles just cover the meat or vegetables with stock. Bear in mind, if using fresh tomatoes, that you will need slightly less stock because the tomatoes will pulp down as they cook.

Depending on the size of your slow-cooker pot you may need to cut down or increase the quantities of ingredients given in the recipes. A medium-sized slow-cooker pot comfortably makes four portions, while a large one makes six to eight portions. Many of the recipes in this book are designed to serve four people, and so are ideal for a medium-sized slow pot.

The slow cooker can also be used as a bain-marie or steamer. Making steamed puddings works very well and you don't need to top it off with boiling water during cooking since there's no chance the water will boil dry.

As a rough guide, if a recipe takes 1 to 2 hours on the stove or in the oven you should cook it in a slow cooker for 3 to 4 hours on the high setting, or 6 to 8 hours on the low. If a recipe takes 2 to 4 hours on the stove or in the oven, cook it in the slow cooker for 4 to 6 hours on high, or for 8 to 12 hours on low.

Can I cook rice and pasta?

Yes, but since they are both starchy foods they can get sticky and gluey if overcooked. Choose easy-cook rice over ordinary rice where available, since some of the starch has been removed during manufacturing, making it less sticky. If making a risotto, add the stock all at once instead of a ladleful at a time.

Cook pasta in a saucepan of boiling water, drain, and stir it into the slow-cooker pot just

before serving. For lasagne, use precooked dried lasagne noodles and cook for no more than 5 to 6¼ hours. Tiny pasta shapes can be added to soups, without cooking first, for the final 15 to 30 minutes of cooking time.

What about dairy foods and shellfish?

Dairy foods, such as milk, heavy cream, and shredded Cheddar-style cheeses, are fine for recipes with short cooking times, or in baked dishes that are cooked for up to 3 to 5 hours on a low setting, or can be stirred into a dish toward the end of cooking so that they have the final 15 to 30 minutes to add richness and flavor. If you cook them for too long they will separate somewhat unattractively.

Shellfish can be added to a dish, but in small quantities only and, again, toward the end of the cooking time, when the other ingredients are already piping hot. Make sure that the shellfish is also piping hot before

serving, so cook it on high, preferably for 15 minutes, then serve. Do not keep dishes containing shellfish warm. If you are using frozen fish, ensure that it is fully defrosted before adding it to the slow-cooker pot.

Can I reheat foods in the slow cooker?

All manufacturers recommend cooking raw foods only in a slow-cooker pot. To reheat a casserole or stew, put it in a saucepan, set it on the stove, and bring it to boiling, stirring, then cook for at least 10 minutes, or until thoroughly reheated and piping hot throughout. Only reheat cooked food once.

remember the basics

- Always add liquid to a slow-cooker pot, ideally hot or boiling water.
- Test food before serving it to ensure it is thoroughly cooked before serving. Chicken or pork should have no pink juices when they are pierced with a small, sharp knife. Beef and lamb should be tender. Fish should flake into even-colored flakes when pressed with a knife.
- Remove the slow-cooker pot from the machine when the dish is cooked using oven mitts to serve.
- Cover any remaining food, allow it to cool, then transfer it to the refrigerator as soon as possible.

Getting the most from your slow cooker

Get ahead

Just 15 minutes' prep is all it takes to get a good meal underway, but trying to do that before you go out to work in the mornings might be a tall order. To make mornings easier, you could prepare meat and vegetables the night before—peeling onions and chopping meat and storing them in the refrigerator in plastic containers, for instance. Marinating foods overnight adds flavor, helps tenderize meat, and saves time next day—you could fry them or add them straight to the slow-cooker pot in the morning with hot stock. Cover, set the temperature, and walk away.

Short of time?

Not all slow cooker recipes take 8 to 10 hours, and plenty can be served in 5 to 6 hours. You can put these on after dropping the kids off at school, so the meal will be ready by pickup time. If shorter cooking times appeal to you, as a quick guide, look for recipes in this book that use a small bone-in roast or that are cooked on the high setting. Or, if you just have two hours and want to share lunch with a friend, choose a risotto or a gently cooked fish dish.

Combining meat and vegetables

Nutritionists and dieticians all recommend that we cut down on the amount of meat we eat. Adding vegetables, canned legumes, and dried lentils to an everyday meaty casserole not only adds essential fiber, vitamins, and minerals, but also helps reduce the meat content of the recipe, which makes it cheaper, too. For fussy eaters, grate or very finely chop vegetables so that they go unnoticed.

Surprisingly, diced root vegetables take as long to cook as meat—and even longer, if they are cut into large chunks. Cut all the root vegetables the same size and, if anything, slightly smaller than the size of the pieces of meat so that they will all be ready at the same time. Remember also to press everything beneath the liquid so that it all cooks evenly.

There's no need to cook crunchy green vegetables like broccoli, spinach, or kale separately. Cut them into small pieces and add them to the slow cooker for the final 15 to 30 minutes of cooking so they stay bright green.

You can use frozen vegetables, such as peas or kernel corn, in a dish, and they don't need to be defrosted first. Just add them in small amounts, so that they don't cool down the liquid too much, for the final 15 to 30 minutes of the cooking time. Increasing the quantity of vegetables helps keep calories low. To cut calories even more, trim off and discard the fat or skin from meat and poultry.

Combined temperatures

Most of the stews and casseroles in the book are cooked on low, but it can be helpful to raise the temperature to high for the final 15 to 60 minutes of cooking time, especially if adding extra vegetables, shrimp, dumplings, or cobbler toppings, or other finishing touches.

Don't be tempted to peek

A slow cooker cooks so gently that there really is no need for you to stir the food since it won't stick or boil dry while it cooks. Don't be tempted to open the lid because every time you do so you release some of the heat, and that can add up to 10 to 15 minutes to the cooking time. It's much better to peer through the glass lid, and stir just once before serving or when adding extra ingredients toward the end of the cooking time.

Thickening

The liquid in a recipe doesn't reduce down during slow cooking, so you may like to add a little thickening agent to the sauce. This can be done either after frying, by sprinkling in a little all-purpose flour to fried onions and meat, or at the end of the cooking time, by stirring in a teaspoonful or two of cornstarch mixed to a paste with water for the final 15 minutes of cooking. For pot roasts, you can strain off or ladle out the liquid at the end of cooking and reduce it by boiling it rapidly in a saucepan for 10 minutes.

Double up

If your family is small, cook the maximum amount that you can in your slow cooker, take out enough for your supper, then cool the remainder and freeze it in handy-sized portions, ready for those days when you don't have time to cook, or the kids need something you can microwave on those days when you arrive home late.

Tips

- Since foods cook so slowly in a slow cooker you can make use of cheaper cuts of beef, such as chuck, brisket, or oxtail—without compromising on flavor. Don't forget lamb shoulder, foreshank, and breast, too. And bear in mind that chicken thighs taste better in the slow cooker than the more expensive chicken breasts!

- Foods will not brown in the slow cooker, so add color to your stews by frying onions and meats first, adding spices or herbs, tomatoes or tomato paste, wine or beer, or browning and seasoning sauce.

- Avoid having to wash extra dishes by pureeing soups while they are still in the slow-cooker pot using a hand-held electric stick blender.

- Getting a steamed pudding out of the slow-cooker pot can be tricky, especially if the pudding mold fits snugly in the pot. Tie string around the mold to make a handle for lifting it out of the slow-cooker pot. Or, fold two pieces of foil individually to make two long straps. Form a cross with the straps and place them on the work surface, then place the steamed pudding mold on the cross and use the pieces of foil to lift up and lower the mold into the slow-cooker pot. Tuck the straps over the top of the mold, then use them to lift out the mold at the end of the cooking time.

- Food sitting at the bottom of the slow-cooker pot will cook more quickly than the rest, so add diced potatoes to the pot first, since these can take longer to cook than meat. Or, if you are adding a lot of root vegetables, cut them into chunks the same size or slightly smaller than the meat you are using and mix up the meat and vegetable chunks.

- Running out of time? Take a shortcut! Add a jar or can of ready-made sauce instead of making your own.

main meal soups

spicy tomato & bean soup

Preparation time **15 minutes**
Cooking temperature **low**
Cooking time **8 to 9 hours**
Serves **4**

1 tablespoon **olive oil**
1 **onion**, chopped
2 **garlic cloves**, minced
½ teaspoon **hot smoked**
   paprika or **chili powder**
1¼ cups **vegetable stock**
2 teaspoons **light brown**
   sugar
½ teaspoon **dried oregano**
1 tablespoon **tomato paste**
1¼ lb **tomatoes**, skinned if
   liked, cut into chunks
14 oz can **cannellini beans**,
   drained
salt and **pepper**
warm **garlic bread**, to serve

Preheat the slow cooker if necessary; see the manufacturer's instructions. Heat the oil in a skillet, add the onion, and fry over medium heat for 4 to 5 minutes, stirring, until the onion is lightly browned. Stir in the garlic and paprika or chili powder.

Pour in the stock and add the sugar, oregano, and tomato paste. Season with salt and pepper and bring to a boil, stirring.

Add the tomatoes and cannellini beans to the slow-cooker pot, then pour in the stock mixture. Stir everything together, then cover and cook on low for 8 to 9 hours or until the vegetables are tender.

Taste and adjust the seasoning, if needed. Ladle into bowls and serve with warm garlic bread.

For spicy tomato & chorizo soup, make the soup as above, omitting the canned beans and adding 2 cups diced potatoes and 3½ oz chorizo sausage, diced, to the slow-cooker pot before pouring in the stock mixture. Cook and serve as above.

cauliflower, leek & stilton soup

Preparation time **25 minutes**
Cooking temperature **high**
Cooking time **3¾ to 5 hours**
Serves **4**

1 tablespoon **olive oil**
2 tablespoons **butter**
1 large **leek**, chopped
2 tablespoons **long-grain
  white rice**
3¾ cups **vegetable stock**
1 **cauliflower**, cut into florets
2 cups **skim milk**
4 oz **Stilton** or other **blue
  cheese**, rind removed,
  cheese crumbled
6 slices **smoked streaky
  bacon**, broiled until crispy,
  to garnish (optional)
salt and **pepper**

Preheat the slow cooker if necessary; see the manufacturer's instructions. Heat the oil and butter in a saucepan, add the leek, and fry gently for 3 to 4 minutes, or until softened. Add the rice and stock, season with salt and pepper, and bring to a boil, stirring.

Add the cauliflower to the slow-cooker pot, pour in the hot stock mixture, cover with the lid, and cook on high for 3 to 4 hours or until the cauliflower is tender.

Puree the soup while it is still in the slow-cooker pot using a stick blender, or transfer to a blender, blend, then pour back into the slow-cooker pot. Stir in the cold milk, then re-cover and cook for 45 to 60 minutes until piping hot. Stir in half the cheese, then ladle into bowls. Scatter with the remaining cheese and garnish with chopped broiled crispy bacon, if liked. Sprinkle with some freshly ground black pepper and serve with warm crusty bread, if liked.

For cauliflower, leek & watercress soup, make the soup as above, adding just 1¼ cups milk. Omit the Stilton or blue cheese and add 1½ cups finely chopped watercress, ½ cup heavy cream, and 1 to 2 teaspoons Dijon mustard (to taste) to the pureed soup. Re-cover and cook in the slow cooker for 30 to 45 minutes. Serve topped with diced grilled bacon.

pumpkin, carrot & quinoa soup

Preparation time **25 minutes**
Cooking temperature **low**
Cooking time **7 to 8 hours**
Serves **4**

1 tablespoon **olive oil**
1 **onion**, chopped
1 ¼ quarts **vegetable stock**
2 teaspoons **harissa paste**,
   plus extra to serve
1 lb **ready-prepared pumpkin**
   or **butternut squash**, cut
   into ¾-inch cubes
2 **carrots**, diced
¼ cup **quinoa**
salt and **pepper**
handful of **cilantro**, coarsely
   chopped, to garnish

Preheat the slow cooker if necessary; see the manufacturer's instructions. Heat the oil in a saucepan, add the onion, and fry for 4 to 5 minutes, stirring, until softened. Pour in the vegetable stock and add the harissa, season with salt and pepper, and bring to a boil, stirring.

Add the pumpkin or squash, carrots, and quinoa to the slow-cooker pot, pour in the hot stock mixture, then cover with the lid and cook on low for 7 to 8 hours or until the vegetables are tender.

Mash the hot soup. Taste and adjust the seasoning, if needed. Ladle into bowls, top with a little extra harissa, and sprinkle with chopped cilantro.

For carrot & rice soup, add 1 ¼ lb carrots, diced, to the slow-cooker pot instead of the mixture of pumpkin and carrots, with ¼ cup long-grain white rice instead of the quinoa. Add 1 teaspoon curry powder and 2 minced garlic cloves to the hot stock mixture instead of the harissa. Cook and serve as above.

beet & apple soup

Preparation time **25 minutes**
Cooking temperature **low**
Cooking time **8 to 9 hours**
Serves **4 to 6**

1 tablespoon **olive oil**
1 **onion**, chopped
1 quart **vegetable stock**
14 oz trimmed **raw beets**,
   peeled and cut into
   ¾-inch cubes
1¼ cups peeled, diced **apple**
salt and **pepper**

Fennel & chile croûtes
½ stick **butter**, at room
   temperature
1 teaspoon **fennel seeds**,
   coarsely crushed
¼ teaspoon **crushed dried
   red chiles**
3 tablespoons chopped
   parsley or **chives**
1 small **French stick**,
   thickly sliced

Preheat the slow cooker if necessary; see the manufacturer's instructions. Heat the oil in a saucepan, add the onion, and fry for 5 minutes, stirring, until softened. Add the stock, season with salt and pepper, and bring to a boil, stirring.

Add the beet cubes and diced apple to the slow-cooker pot. Pour in the hot stock mixture. Cover and cook on low for 8 to 9 hours or until the beet cubes are tender.

Meanwhile, mix the butter with the fennel seeds, chiles, and chopped herbs. Put the mixture into a small dish, cover, and chill until needed.

Puree the soup using a stick blender in the slow-cooker pot, or transfer the mixture to a blender and puree, then pour it back into the slow-cooker pot. Taste and adjust the seasoning, if needed. Toast the bread, then spread with the flavored butter. Ladle the hot soup into bowls, float the croûtes on top, and serve immediately.

For beet & carrot soup with herb croûtes,

omit the apple and add 2 cups diced carrots. Cook as above. For the croûtes, mix ½ stick butter with 3 tablespoons mixed fresh chopped herbs only, then spread the flavored butter onto the sliced toasted French stick as above.

vegetable broth with dumplings

Preparation time **35 minutes**
Cooking temperature **low**
Cooking time **8¾ to 11 hours**
Serves **4**

3 tablespoons **butter**
1 **leek**, sliced, white and green
    parts kept separate
1 cup diced **turnips**
1 cup diced **parsnips**
1 cup diced **carrots**,
1 **celery stalk**, sliced
¼ cup **pearl barley**
1 quart **boiling vegetable** or
    chicken stock
2 to 3 **sage sprigs**
1 teaspoon **English mustard**
salt and **pepper**

Dumplings
½ cup **all-purpose flour**
    sifted with ½ teaspoon
    baking powder
¼ cup **vegetable shortening**
2 **strips bacon**, finely diced
about 3 tablespoons **water**

Preheat the slow cooker if necessary; see the manufacturer's instructions. Heat the butter in a large skillet, add the white leek slices, reserving the green slices, and fry for 2 to 3 minutes until softened. Stir in the root vegetables and celery and fry for 4 to 5 minutes.

Add the pearl barley to the slow-cooker pot, then add the fried vegetables, boiling stock, and sage. Stir in the mustard and a little salt and pepper. Cover with the lid and cook on low for 8 to 10 hours or until the vegetables and barley are tender.

Make the dumplings. Put the flour and baking powder mixture, shortening, bacon, and a little salt and pepper into a bowl and mix well. Gradually stir in enough of the measurement water to make a soft but not sticky dough. Knead lightly on a floured surface, then shape into 12 balls.

Stir the reserved green leek slices into the soup, add the dumplings, spacing them slightly apart, then re-cover and continue to cook for 45 to 60 minutes or until light and fluffy. Ladle into bowls and serve.

For chicken broth with mini herb dumplings, fry 4 small chicken thighs on the bone with the white leek slices. Add the root vegetables and celery, omitting the parsnips. Continue and cook as above for 8 to 10 hours. Make the dumplings with 2 tablespoons mixed chopped parsley or chives and sage instead of the bacon. Lift the chicken out of the soup, discard the skin and bones, and chop the meat into small pieces. Return the meat to the pot with the raw dumplings and green leeks, re-cover, and cook for 45 to 60 minutes.

spiced parsnip & red lentil soup

Preparation time **25 minutes**
Cooking temperature **low**
Cooking time **7 to 8 hours**
Serves **4**

2 tablespoons **butter**
1 tablespoon **olive oil**
1 **onion**, chopped
1 **garlic clove**, minced
1 teaspoon **ground coriander**
½ teaspoon **ground cumin**
½ teaspoon **turmeric**
1 quart **vegetable stock**
1 lb **parsnips**, cut into chunks
¼ cup **red lentils**
salt and **pepper**

To serve
½ cup **heavy cream**
2 tablespoons **sweet
   chili sauce**

Preheat the slow cooker if necessary; see the manufacturer's instructions. Heat the butter and oil in a saucepan, add the onion, and fry for 5 minutes, stirring, until softened. Stir in the garlic and spices, then mix in the stock. Add a little salt and pepper and bring to a boil, stirring constantly.

Add the parsnips and red lentils to the slow-cooker pot. Pour in the hot stock mixture, then cover with the lid and cook on low for 7 to 8 hours until the parsnips and lentils are tender.

Puree with a stick blender in the slow-cooker pot or transfer to a blender, blend, then return the mixture to the slow-cooker pot. Taste and adjust the seasoning, if needed. Ladle into bowls, drizzle with the cream and chili sauce, and serve immediately.

For sweet potato & red lentil soup with ginger,
fry the onion in the butter as above, stir in the spices, then add a 1½-inch piece of peeled and finely chopped fresh ginger root with the garlic. Add 1 lb peeled sweet potatoes, cut into chunks, in place of the parsnips to the slow-cooker pot with the lentils. Add the remaining ingredients and cook as above. Puree with a handful of cilantro leaves and serve with just a swirl of cream.

garlicky eggplant & spinach soup

Preparation time **20 minutes**
Cooking temperature **high**
  and **low**
Cooking time **5¼ to 6¼ hours**
Serves **4**

2 tablespoons **olive oil**
1 **onion**, finely chopped
1 **eggplant**, cut into small
  cubes
1½ cups diced **potato**
2 **garlic cloves**, minced
1 teaspoon **ground cumin**
1 teaspoon **ground coriander**
½ cup **green lentils**
juice of 1 **lemon**
1 quart **boiling vegetable
  stock**
4 oz **baby spinach**, larger
  leaves torn into pieces
salt and **pepper**

Preheat the slow cooker if necessary; see the manufacturer's instructions. Heat the oil in a large skillet, add the onion and eggplant, and fry for 5 minutes, stirring, until softened and lightly browned.

Stir in the potato, garlic, and ground spices, then add to the slow-cooker pot. Add the lentils and lemon juice, then pour in the hot stock. Season with a little salt and pepper, then cover with the lid and cook on high for 5 to 6 hours or until the lentils are tender.

Add the spinach leaves, pressing them beneath the liquid, re-cover the slow cooker, and cook on low for 15 minutes, until the spinach has just wilted and is still bright green in color. Taste and adjust the seasoning, if needed. Ladle into bowls and serve with warm crusty bread, if liked.

For curried eggplant & spinach soup, fry the onion and eggplant as above. Add the potato, garlic, and 4 teaspoons mild curry paste or powder instead of the ground spices. Add the lentils, a 14 oz can diced tomatoes, and just 2½ cups boiling vegetable stock. Omit the lemon juice and cook as above, adding the spinach for the last 15 minutes of cooking, as above.

salmon in hot miso broth

Preparation time **20 minutes**
Cooking temperature **low**
and **high**
Cooking time **1 hour
40 minutes to 2 hours
10 minutes**
Serves **6**

4 **salmon steaks**, about
4 oz each
1 **carrot**, thinly sliced
4 **scallions**, thinly sliced
2 cups thinly sliced **white
mushrooms**
1 large **red chile,** halved,
seeded, and finely chopped
¾-inch **piece of fresh
ginger root,** peeled and
finely chopped
3 tablespoons **miso**
1 tablespoon **dark soy sauce**
2 tablespoons **mirin** (optional)
1¼ quarts **boiling fish stock**
¾ cup thinly sliced **snow peas**
cilantro leaves, to garnish

Preheat the slow cooker if necessary; see the manufacturer's instructions. Rinse the salmon in cold water, drain, and place in the slow-cooker pot. Arrange the carrot, scallions, mushrooms, chile, and ginger on top of the fish.

Add the miso, soy sauce, and mirin, if using, to the boiling stock and stir until the miso has dissolved. Pour the stock mixture over the salmon and vegetables. Cover with the lid and cook on low for 1½ to 2 hours or until the fish is tender and the soup is piping hot.

Lift out the fish with a slotted spoon or lifter and transfer it to a plate. Flake it into chunky pieces, discarding the skin and any bones. Return the fish to the slow-cooker pot and add the snow peas. Re-cover and cook on high for 10 minutes or until the snow peas are just tender, then ladle the soup into bowls. Garnish with the cilantro leaves to serve.

For salmon in aromatic Thai broth, follow the recipe as above, adding 3 teaspoons Thai red curry paste, 3 small kaffir lime leaves, and 2 teaspoons fish sauce instead of the miso and mirin.

minestrone primavera

Preparation time **20 minutes**
Cooking temperature **high**
Cooking time **5½ to 7 hours**
Serves **4**

1 **chicken carcass**
1 **onion**, cut into chunks
2 **carrots**, thickly sliced
2 **rosemary sprigs**
2 **bay leaves**
1½ quarts **boiling water**
1½ cups skinned (if liked),
   and diced **tomatoes**
1 **red bell pepper**, cored,
   seeded, and diced
3 oz **purple sprouting
   broccoli**, thinly sliced
¾ cup **romano green beans**,
   thinly sliced
¾ cup small **pasta shells**
handful of **basil**, finely
   chopped
salt and **pepper**
shredded **Parmesan cheese**,
   to serve

Preheat the slow cooker if necessary; see the manufacturer's instructions. Tear the chicken carcass in half, then add it to the slow-cooker pot with the onion, carrots, and herbs. Pour the boiling water over the ingredients in the pot and season with salt and pepper.

Cover with the lid and cook on high for 5 to 6 hours. Strain the stock and return it immediately to the slow-cooker pot and re-cover. Strip any meat from the carcass, then add it to the slow-cooker pot along with the tomatoes, red bell pepper, broccoli, romano green beans, and pasta.

Re-cover and cook for 30 to 60 minutes or until the vegetables are tender. Stir in the basil, taste, and adjust the seasoning, if needed. Ladle into bowls and sprinkle with a little shredded Parmesan. Serve with a warm French stick, if liked.

For minestrone verde, make the soup as above, replacing the red bell pepper with 1 cored, seeded, and diced green bell pepper. Add 3½ oz spinach, finely shredded, for the final 10 minutes of cooking.

chicken noodle broth

Preparation time **10 minutes**
Cooking temperature **high**
Cooking time **5 hours**
   20 minutes to 7½ hours
Serves **4**

1 **chicken carcass**
1 **onion**, cut into wedges
2 **carrots**, sliced
2 **celery stalks**, sliced
1 **bouquet garni**
1¼ quarts **boiling water**
3 oz **vermicelli noodles**
¼ cup chopped **parsley**
salt and **pepper**

Preheat the slow cooker if necessary; see the manufacturer's instructions. Place the chicken carcass in the slow-cooker pot, tearing it into 2 pieces if necessary to make it fit. Add the onion, carrots, celery, and bouquet garni. Pour in the boiling water and season to taste. Cover and cook on high for 5 to 7 hours until the vegetables are tender.

Strain the soup through a large sieve, then return the liquid to the slow-cooker pot. Remove any meat from the carcass and add it to the pot. Adjust the seasoning if necessary, add the pasta, and cook for a further 20 to 30 minutes until the pasta is just cooked. Sprinkle with the parsley, ladle into deep bowls, and serve.

For chicken, pea & mint soup, follow the recipe above to make the soup, omitting the pasta, then strain and pour it back into the slow-cooker pot. Add 2 cups finely sliced leeks, 2½ cups frozen peas, and a small bunch of mint, re-cover, and cook for a further 30 minutes. Puree the soup in a blender or with a hand-held stick blender, then stir in 5 oz mascarpone cheese until melted. Ladle into bowls and scatter with extra mint, if liked.

country mushroom & bacon soup

Preparation time **20 minutes**
Cooking temperature **low**
Cooking time **8 hours**
   5 minutes to 9 hours
   10 minutes
Serves **4**

2 tablespoons **butter**
1 tablespoon **olive oil**
1 **onion**, chopped
4 strips **smoked bacon**, diced
3¾ cups **vegetable stock**
1 tablespoon **balsamic
   vinegar**
4¼ cups sliced **white
   mushrooms**
½ oz **dried mixed
   mushrooms**, larger
   pieces sliced
1½ cups diced **potatoes**
¼ cup **pearl barley**
2 **thyme sprigs**
½ cup **heavy cream**
few extra **thyme leaves** or
   a little chopped **parsley**,
   to garnish
salt and **pepper**

Preheat the slow cooker if necessary; see the manufacturer's instructions. Heat the butter and oil in a saucepan, add the onion and bacon, and fry over medium heat for 5 minutes, stirring, until lightly browned.

Pour in the stock, add the balsamic vinegar, then season well with salt and pepper and bring to a boil, stirring.

Add the fresh and dried mushrooms to the slow-cooker pot, then add the potato, barley, and thyme. Pour the hot stock mixture into the slow cooker and stir together. Cover and cook on low for 8 to 9 hours until the bacon and vegetables are tender.

Stir in the cream, taste, and adjust the seasoning, if needed. Re-cover and cook for 5 to 10 minutes until the cream is heated through. Ladle into shallow bowls, discarding the thyme sprigs and adding a few extra thyme leaves or a little chopped parsley. Serve with warm crusty bread, if liked.

For country vegetable & bacon soup, fry the onion and bacon as above. Add the stock and seasoning and omit the vinegar. Add a mixture of diced turnips, carrots, leeks, and fresh mushrooms (about 2¼ cups), then the dried mushrooms and remaining ingredients. Cook and serve as above.

chunky chickpea & chorizo soup

Preparation time **20 minutes**
Cooking temperature **low**
Cooking time **6 to 8 hours**
Serves **4**

2 tablespoons **olive oil**
1 **onion**, chopped
2 **garlic cloves**, mixed
5 oz **chorizo sausage**, diced
½ teaspoon **hot smoked paprika**
2 to 3 **thyme sprigs**
1 quart **chicken stock**
1 tablespoon **tomato paste**
2¾ cups peeled and diced **sweet potatoes**
14½ oz can **chickpeas**, drained
salt and **pepper**
chopped **parsley** or extra **thyme leaves**, to garnish

Preheat the slow cooker if necessary; see the manufacturer's instructions. Heat the oil in a skillet, add the onion, and fry, stirring, for 5 minutes or until just beginning to turn golden.

Stir in the garlic and chorizo sausage and cook for 2 minutes. Mix in the paprika, add the thyme, stock, and tomato paste, and bring to a boil, stirring constantly, then season with a little salt and pepper.

Add the sweet potatoes and chickpeas to the slow-cooker pot and pour in the hot stock mixture. Cover with the lid and cook on low for 6 to 8 hours until the sweet potatoes are tender.

Ladle into bowls, scatter with a little chopped parsley or extra thyme, and serve with warm pitta bread, if liked.

For tomato, chickpea & chorizo soup, make the soup as above up to the point where the paprika and thyme have been added. Reduce the stock to 3¼ cups and add to the skillet with the tomato paste and 2 teaspoons brown sugar. Bring to a boil. Omit the sweet potatoes but add 1 lb skinned and diced tomatoes to the slow-cooker pot along with the chickpeas. Pour in the stock mixture and continue as above.

rustic sausage & kale soup

Preparation time **25 minutes**
Cooking temperature **low**
Cooking time **8 hours**
  20 minutes to 9½ hours
Serves **4**

2 tablespoons **olive oil**
6 **garlicky Toulouse-style
  sausages**, about 14 oz in
  total, thickly sliced
1 **onion**, chopped
2 cups cubed **potatoes**
2 **carrots**, diced
14 oz can **diced tomatoes**
1 tablespoon **balsamic
  vinegar**
2 cups **chicken**
  or **pork stock**
2 **rosemary sprigs**
8 oz package **ready-cooked
  green lentils**, drained
  if needed
3½ oz shredded **green kale**
salt and **pepper**

Preheat the slow cooker if necessary; see the manufacturer's instructions. Heat the oil in a saucepan, add the sausages, and fry over medium heat for 5 minutes until they are just beginning to brown. Stir in the onion, potato, and carrot and cook for a further 5 minutes until the vegetables are beginning to soften.

Pour in the tomatoes, vinegar, and stock, then add the rosemary and salt and pepper. Bring to a boil, stirring.

Tip the lentils into the bottom of the slow-cooker pot. Pour in the hot tomato mixture, then press the sausages and vegetables beneath the liquid. Cover and cook on low for 8 to 9 hours or until the potatoes are tender and the sausages are cooked through.

Stir in the kale, re-cover the slow cooker, and cook for 20 to 30 minutes until the kale is bright green and just tender. Taste and adjust the seasoning, if needed. Ladle into shallow bowls and serve with hot garlic bread, if liked.

For rustic sausage & pea soup, make the soup as above using 6 pork sausages flavored with herbs instead of the garlicky Toulouse-style sausages. Add ½ cup frozen peas instead of the kale, re-cover, and cook for 20 to 30 minutes on low.

harira

Preparation time **20 minutes**
Cooking temperature **high**
Cooking time **5 to 6 hours**
Serves **4**

1 tablespoon **olive oil**
1 **onion**, chopped
2 **garlic cloves**, minced
1 teaspoon **mild paprika**
1 teaspoon **turmeric**
½ teaspoon **ground cumin**
½ teaspoon **ground
   cinnamon**
2½ cups **lamb stock**
1 tablespoon **tomato paste**
¾ lb **lamb shank**
1 **potato**, diced
2 **celery stalks**, diced
2 **carrots**, diced
2 cups skinned (if liked),
   diced **tomatoes**
14 oz can **chickpeas**, drained
salt and **pepper**

To garnish
handful of **mint**,coarsely
   chopped
handful of **parsley**, coarsely
   chopped

Preheat the slow cooker if necessary; see the manufacturer's instructions. Heat the oil in a saucepan, add the onion, and fry for 5 minutes, stirring, until softened. Stir in the garlic and spices and cook for 1 minute.

Pour in the stock, add the tomato paste, and season with salt and pepper. Bring to a boil, stirring.

Add the lamb shank to the slow-cooker pot with the potato, celery, carrots, and tomatoes, then pour in the drained chickpeas.

Pour the hot stock mixture into the slow-cooker pot. Cover and cook on high for 5 to 6 hours or until the lamb is beginning to fall off of the bone.

Lift the lamb out of the slow-cooker pot, take the meat off of the bone, cut it into small pieces, discarding any fat, then return it to the slow-cooker pot. Scatter with the chopped herbs, taste, and adjust the seasoning, if needed. Ladle into bowls and serve with warm crusty bread, if liked.

For vegetable harira, omit the lamb shank and lamb stock and replace with 2½ cups vegetable stock and 1 red bell pepper, cored, seeded, and diced. Cook as above, then add 1 cup frozen fava or edamame beans for the final 20 to 30 minutes of cooking.

kids'
favorites

baked tuna & pasta

Preparation time **30 minutes**
Cooking temperature **low**
Cooking time **5 to 6 hours**
Serves **4**

1 tablespoon **olive oil**
1 **onion**, chopped
2 **garlic cloves**, minced
1 **red bell pepper**, cored,
    seeded, and diced
1 **green bell pepper**, cored,
    seeded, and diced
2 **celery stalks**, diced
14 oz can **diced tomatoes**
½ cup **vegetable stock**
1 tablespoon **tomato paste**
2 teaspoons **superfine sugar**
7 oz can **tuna in springwater**,
    drained
handful of **basil leaves**, plus
    extra to garnish
8 oz **dried pasta twists**
7 oz **mozzarella cheese**
freshly shredded **Parmesan**
    cheese
salt and **pepper**

Preheat the slow cooker if necessary; see the manufacturer's instructions. Heat the oil in a skillet, add the onion, and fry for 5 minutes until softened. Stir in the garlic, diced bell peppers, and celery.

Mix in the diced tomatoes, stock, tomato paste, and sugar and season with salt and pepper. Bring to a boil, stirring.

Pour the sauce into the slow-cooker pot, add the tuna, broken into chunky pieces, and scatter in some of the basil leaves, torn into pieces. Cover with the lid and cook on low for 5 to 6 hours until the tuna is tender.

When almost ready, add the pasta to a saucepan of boiling water, cook for 8 to 10 minutes until just tender, then drain. Stir the pasta into the tuna sauce and scatter with the mozzarella, drained and torn into pieces, a little shredded Parmesan, and a few of the smallest basil leaves. If liked, you can then lift out the cooking pot using oven mitts and brown the top under a preheated hot broiler. Scatter with extra basil leaves to serve.

For baked chicken & pasta, add 1 lb raw chicken breast strips, cut into small pieces, in place of the canned tuna and cook on low for 8 to 9 hours until the chicken is thoroughly cooked through. Serve as above.

chicken, tomato & pesto hotpot

Preparation time **30 minutes**
Cooking temperature **high**
Cooking time **6 to 7 hours**
Serves **4**

1 tablespoon **olive oil**
1 ¼ lb **boneless, skinless chicken thighs,**
cut into chunks
1 **onion**, chopped
1 tablespoon **all-purpose flour**
2 **garlic cloves**, minced
1 **red bell pepper**, cored, seeded, and diced
1 **yellow bell pepper**, cored, seeded, and diced
1 ¼ cups sliced **button mushrooms**
14 oz can **diced tomatoes**
1 ¼ cups **chicken stock**
2 teaspoons **pesto**
1 ¼ lb **potatoes**, thinly sliced
1 ½ tablespoons **butter** (optional)
salt and **pepper**

Preheat the slow cooker if necessary; see the manufacturer's instructions. Heat the oil in a saucepan, add the chicken and onion, and fry for 5 minutes, stirring, until the chicken is lightly browned.

Stir in the flour, then mix in the garlic, bell peppers, and mushrooms. Add the tomatoes, stock, and 1 teaspoon of the pesto, then season with salt and pepper and bring to a boil, stirring.

Transfer to the slow-cooker pot. Place the potato slices on top, arranging them so they overlap, then press them lightly into the stock. Spread the potatoes with the remaining pesto and a little extra salt and pepper, then cover with the lid and cook on high for 6 to 7 hours or until the potatoes are tender when pierced with a knife.

Serve as it is, or dot the top of the potatoes with the butter, then lift the slow-cooker pot out of the machine using oven mitts and brown the tops of the potatoes under a preheated hot broiler. Serve with steamed green snap beans, if liked.

For chicken, tomato & bacon hotpot, fry the chicken and onion with 4 oz diced bacon. Add the garlic, bell peppers, and mushrooms, then the tomatoes, stock, and 1 teaspoon mixed dried herbs instead of the pesto. Add the potato topping and scatter with a little extra dried herbs. Cook as above and garnish with fresh chopped parsley.

chicken & chorizo risotto

Preparation time **20 minutes**
Cooking temperature **low**
Cooking time **6 to 7¼ hours**
Serves **4**

1 tablespoon **olive oil**
1 lb **boneless, skinless
  chicken thighs**, diced
3½ oz **chorizo sausage**,
  diced
2 **garlic cloves**, minced
1 **red bell pepper**, cored,
  seeded, and sliced
1 **yellow bell pepper**, cored,
  seeded, and sliced
2 **rosemary sprigs**
1¼ quarts **boiling chicken
  stock**
1¼ cups **risotto rice**
1 cup **frozen peas**
salt and **pepper**
shredded **Cheddar or
  Parmesan cheese**, to serve
  (optional)

Preheat the slow cooker if necessary; see the manufacturer's instructions. Heat the oil in a skillet, add the chicken, and fry for 4 to 5 minutes, stirring, until just beginning to brown. Mix in the chorizo and garlic and cook for 2 minutes.

Tip the chicken mixture into the slow-cooker pot, then add the bell peppers and rosemary. Pour in the boiling stock, season with salt and pepper, and stir together.

Cover and cook on low for 5 to 6 hours until the chicken is cooked through. Stir in the risotto rice, cover, and cook for 45 to 60 minutes. Stir in the frozen peas, re-cover, and cook for 15 minutes until the peas are hot and the rice is tender. Discard the rosemary. Spoon the risotto into shallow bowls and top with a little shredded cheese, if liked.

For turkey & bacon risotto, replace the chicken with 1 lb diced, skinless turkey breast meat and the chorizo sausage with 4 oz diced smoked Canadian bacon. Add the remaining ingredients and make the risotto as above.

chicken & mango curry

Preparation time **25 minutes**
Cooking temperature **low**
Cooking time **8 to 9 hours**
Serves **4**

2 **onions**, quartered
1 **apple**, cored
2-inch piece of **fresh ginger
root**, peeled and sliced
2 **garlic cloves**, halved
2 tablespoons **butter**
3 tablespoons **korma
curry paste**
3 tablespoons **mango
chutney**
1 teaspoon **turmeric**
1 ½ lb **boneless, skinless
chicken thighs**, cubed
¼ cup **red lentils**
2 cups **boiling chicken stock**
½ cup **heavy cream**
salt and **pepper**

Preheat the slow cooker if necessary; see the manufacturer's instructions. Finely chop the onion, apple, ginger root, and garlic in a food processor, if you have one, or using a large knife.

Heat the butter in a skillet, add the onion mixture, and fry gently for 3 to 4 minutes until softened. Stir in the curry paste, chutney, and turmeric, then season with a little salt and pepper.

Add the chicken and lentils to the slow-cooker pot, spoon the onion mixture over the top, then pour in the boiling chicken stock and mix together. Press the pieces of chicken beneath the liquid, then cover with the lid and cook on low for 8 to 9 hours until the chicken is cooked through and the lentils are soft.

Stir the cream into the curry, then spoon into shallow dishes and serve accompanied by steamed basmati rice, if liked, and topped with spoonfuls of mango sambal, if liked (see below).

For mango sambal, to serve as an accompaniment, mix together 1 mango, cut in 3 and seeded, diced, and peeled, 2 finely chopped scallions, 5 oz dried coconut shavings, the grated zest and juice of 1 lime, ½ or a whole seeded and very finely chopped red chile (to taste), and a small handful of cilantro, finely chopped.

spicy turkey tortillas

Preparation time **20 minutes**
Cooking temperature **low**
Cooking time **8 to 10 hours**
Serves **4**

1 tablespoon **olive oil**
13 oz **ground turkey breast**
1 **onion**, chopped
2 **garlic cloves**, minced
1 teaspoon **crushed red chile flakes**
1 teaspoon **cumin seeds**, crushed
1 teaspoon **mild paprika**
14 oz can **diced tomatoes**
7 oz can **red kidney beans**, drained
½ cup **chicken stock**
1 tablespoon **tomato paste**
1 **red bell pepper**, cored, seeded, and diced
salt and **pepper**

To serve
4 x 8-inch **soft tortilla wraps**
2 oz **salad leaves**
¼ cup **Greek-style yogurt**
½ cup shredded **Cheddar cheese**
fresh cilantro leaves, torn

Preheat the slow cooker if necessary; see the manufacturer's instructions. Put the oil into a large skillet and place the pan over high heat until hot. Add the ground turkey and onion and fry for 4 to 5 minutes, stirring and breaking up the turkey with a wooden spoon, until it is just beginning to brown.

Stir in the garlic, crushed chile flakes, cumin seeds, and paprika, then add the tomatoes, kidney beans, stock, and tomato paste. Add the red bell pepper, season with salt and pepper, and bring to a boil. Transfer to the slow-cooker pot, cover, and cook on low for 8 to 10 hours until the turkey is cooked through.

Warm the tortillas for 1 to 2 minutes on each side in a hot, dry skillet, then place on 4 serving plates. Spoon the spicy turkey on top, then add a handful of salad leaves to each, a spoonful of yogurt, a little Cheddar, and top with some torn cilantro. Serve immediately.

For spicy turkey with mashed potato topping, follow the recipe above to make and cook the spicy turkey mixture. Cook, drain, and mash 1 ½ lb potatoes, stir in ¼ cup vegetable stock, and season to taste. Place the turkey mixture in a shallow baking dish and spoon the mashed potato on top. Rough up the top with a fork, then brush with ½ beaten egg. Brown under the broiler before serving.

monday sausage stew

Preparation time **20 minutes**
Cooking temperature **low**
Cooking time **7 to 8 hours**
Serves **4**

1 lb small, thin **pork sausages**
1 **onion**, chopped
2 x 14 oz cans **baked beans**
2 tablespoons **Worcestershire
sauce**
1 teaspoon **dried mixed
herbs**
1 teaspoon **Dijon mustard**
1 cup **boiling chicken stock**
10 oz **ready-prepared
pumpkin** or **butternut
squash**, cut into
¾-inch cubes
salt and **pepper**

Preheat the slow cooker if necessary; see the manufacturer's instructions. Broil the sausages on one side only.

Meanwhile, add the onion, baked beans, and Worcestershire sauce to the slow-cooker pot. Stir in the herbs, mustard, and boiling stock, then mix in the pumpkin or squash. Season with salt and pepper.

Arrange the sausages on top, with the browned sides uppermost. Press them into the liquid, then cover with the lid and cook on low for 7 to 8 hours until the sausages are cooked through and the pumpkin or squash is tender. Spoon into shallow bowls and serve with garlic bread, if liked.

For sausage stew with chiles, broil 1 lb pork sausages flavored with chile or use small, thin plain pork sausages. Add the onion and 2 x 14 oz cans beans flavored with chili sauce to the slow-cooker pot, omitting the Worcestershire sauce, dried herbs, and Dijon mustard. Mix in the boiling stock and pumpkin or squash and cook as above. Garnish with 3 tablespoons chopped parsley.

sticky ribs

Preparation time **20 minutes**
Cooking temperature **high**
Cooking time **5 to 6 hours**
Serves **4**

2¾ lb **pork ribs**
1 **onion**, quartered
2 **carrots**, thickly sliced
1 teaspoon **dried mixed herbs**
2 tablespoons **malt vinegar**
1 quart **boiling water**
salt and **pepper**

Glaze
2 tablespoons **tomato ketchup**
2 tablespoons **honey**
2 tablespoons **Worcestershire sauce**
1 teaspoon **Dijon mustard**

Preheat the slow cooker if necessary; see the manufacturer's instructions. Add the ribs, onion, and carrots to the slow-cooker pot, then scatter with the dried herbs. Mix the vinegar into the boiling water, pour the mixture into the pot, then season with salt and pepper.

Cover and cook on high for 5 to 6 hours or until the meat is almost falling off the bone.

Line the broiler pan with foil, lift the ribs out of the slow-cooker pot with a slotted spoon, arrange them in a single layer on the foil, then add a ladleful of the cooking liquid.

Mix the tomato ketchup, honey, Worcestershire sauce, and mustard together, then brush the mixture evenly all over the ribs. Cook under a medium broiler for 10 minutes, turning and brushing once or twice until covered with a sticky glaze.

Arrange the ribs on serving plates and serve with coleslaw and baked beans, if liked.

For cola ribs, bring 1 quart cola to a boil in a saucepan, then pour it over the ribs and vegetables instead of the vinegar and boiling water. Cover, cook, and glaze as in the recipe above.

sausage tagliatelle

Preparation time **25 minutes**
Cooking temperature **low**
Cooking time **8 to 10 hours**
Serves **4**

1 tablespoon **sunflower oil**
8 **chile-flavored** or **spicy sausages**
1 **onion**, chopped
2 cups sliced **white mushrooms**
2 **garlic cloves**, minced
14 oz can **diced tomatoes**
½ cup **beef stock**
8 oz **tagliatelle**
salt and **pepper**
basil leaves, to garnish

Preheat the slow cooker if necessary; see the manufacturer's instructions. Heat the oil in a large skillet, add the sausages, and fry, turning, until browned but not cooked through. Transfer the sausages to the slow-cooker pot using tongs.

Drain off all the excess fat from the skillet, leaving about 2 teaspoons behind in the pan, then add the onion and fry until softened. Add the mushrooms and garlic and fry for 1 to 2 minutes.

Stir in the diced tomatoes, stock, and a little salt and pepper and bring to a boil, stirring. Pour the mixture evenly over the sausages, cover with the lid, and cook on low for 8 to 10 hours until the sausages are cooked through.

Bring a large saucepan of water to a boil. Add the tagliatelle and cook for 7 to 8 minutes or until just tender, then drain. Lift the sausages out of the slow-cooker pot and slice thickly, then return them to the pot with the pasta and mix together. Scatter with torn basil leaves and shredded Parmesan, if liked.

For chicken & chorizo tagliatelle, omit the sausages and fry 1 lb diced boneless chicken thighs in 1 tablespoon olive oil until golden. Drain and transfer to the slow-cooker pot. Continue as above, adding 3½ oz chorizo sausage, diced, to the skillet with the onions and replacing the beef stock with ½ cup chicken stock.

spanish meatballs

Preparation time **20 minutes**
Cooking temperature **low**
Cooking time **8¼ to 9¼ hours**
Serves **4**

1 tablespoon **olive oil**
1 **onion,** chopped
3 oz **chorizo sausage**, diced
1 teaspoon **mild paprika**
½ teaspoon **ground cumin**
14 oz can **diced tomatoes**
1 cup **chicken stock**
2 x 13-oz packages containing
    12 fresh **turkey meatballs**
1 cup **frozen peas**
salt and **pepper**

Preheat the slow cooker if necessary; see the manufacturer's instructions. Heat the oil in a saucepan, add the onion and chorizo, and fry for 5 minutes until the onions are golden. Stir in the paprika and cumin, then the tomatoes and stock. Season with salt and pepper and bring to a boil, stirring.

Add the meatballs to the slow-cooker pot and pour in the hot sauce. Cover and cook on low for 8 to 9 hours until the meatballs are cooked through.

Stir the meatballs and scatter the frozen peas over the top, re-cover, and cook for 15 minutes. Gently stir the meatballs again, then serve spooned into rice-lined bowls, if liked.

For spicy beef meatballs, fry the onion with 2 cups sliced white mushrooms, omitting the chorizo. Add the spices, tomatoes, 1 cup beef stock, and seasoning. Add 2 packages containing 12 fresh beef meatballs to the slow-cooker pot, then pour the hot sauce evenly over them. Cook as above, adding the peas, and serve with cooked spaghetti and a little chopped basil.

take 5 spaghetti bolognese

Preparation time **25 minutes**
Cooking temperature **low**
Cooking time **8 to 9 hours**
Serves **4**

1 tablespoon **olive oil**
1 lb **lean ground beef**
1 **onion**, chopped
2 cups **tomato puree**
2 **garlic cloves**, minced
1 **zucchini**, coarsely grated
1 **carrot**, coarsely grated
1 **red bell pepper**, cored,
    seeded, and diced
2 cups chopped **mushrooms**
1 cup **beef stock**
1 teaspoon **dried oregano**
8 oz **dried spaghetti**
salt and **pepper**
small handful of **basil leaves**,
    to garnish

Preheat the slow cooker if necessary; see the manufacturer's instructions. Heat the oil in a saucepan, add the ground beef and onion, and fry for 5 minutes, stirring, until the beef is evenly browned.

Stir in the tomato puree, garlic, and the grated and chopped vegetables, then mix in the stock and oregano and season with salt and pepper. Bring to a boil, stirring.

Pour the mixture into the slow-cooker pot. Press the meat and vegetables into the liquid to submerge them, then cover with the lid and cook on low for 8 to 9 hours until the beef and vegetables are tender.

Once the bolognese sauce is ready, bring a saucepan of water to a boil, add the spaghetti, and cook for 8 to 10 minutes or until tender. Drain, then stir the pasta into the Bolognese sauce. Spoon into shallow bowls and garnish with basil leaves and shredded Parmesan, if liked.

For turkey Bolognese, omit the beef and fry 1 lb ground turkey leg or breast meat with the onion. Add the remaining ingredients, using 1 ¼ cups chicken stock instead of the beef stock. Cook and serve as above.

cheese-topped cottage pie

Preparation time **35 minutes**
Cooking temperature **low**
Cooking time **8 to 9 hours**
Serves **4**

1 tablespoon **sunflower oil**
1 lb **lean ground beef**
1 **onion**, chopped
3 cups mixed diced **carrots**
  and **turnips**
14 oz can **baked beans**
1 ¼ cups **beef stock**
1 tablespoon **Worcestershire**
  sauce
1 teaspoon **dried mixed herbs**
2 lb **potatoes**, cut into chunks
½ stick **butter**
1 **egg**, beaten
3 to 4 tablespoons **milk**
½ cup shredded **Cheddar**
  cheese
salt and **pepper**

Preheat the slow cooker if necessary; see the manufacturer's instructions. Heat the oil in a saucepan, add the ground beef and onion, and fry for 5 minutes, stirring constantly, until the beef is evenly browned.

Stir in the diced vegetables, baked beans, stock, and Worcestershire sauce, then mix in the herbs and season with salt and pepper. Bring to a boil, stirring.

Spoon the mixture into the slow-cooker pot, cover with the lid, and cook on low for 8 to 9 hours until the beef and vegetables are tender.

When you are almost ready to serve, add the potatoes to a saucepan of boiling water, cook for 15 minutes or until tender, then drain and return to the pan. Mash well, then mix in the butter, beaten egg, and enough of the milk to make a smooth consistency. Stir in two-thirds of the cheese and season with salt and pepper.

Transfer the beef mixture from the slow cooker to 4 individual baking dishes, spoon the mashed potatoes evenly on top, rough up the surface with a fork, and scatter with the remaining cheese. Cook under a preheated hot broiler until the cheese is bubbling and golden. Serve with peas, if liked.

For cheese-topped turkey pie, omit the beef and fry 1 lb ground turkey leg or breast meat with the onion as above. Stir in the diced vegetables, baked beans, 1 ¼ cups chicken stock, and the Worcestershire sauce, then mix in the herbs and season. Continue as above.

jumbo burger with tomato sauce

Preparation time **25 minutes**
Cooking temperature **high**
Cooking time **3 to 4 hours**
Serves **4**

oil, for greasing
1 bunch of **scallions**,
  chopped, divided
½ lb **lean ground beef**
½ lb **lean sausages flavored
  with herbs**, casing removed
¼ cup **fresh bread crumbs**
2 tablespoons **Worcestershire
  sauce**, divided
14 oz can **diced tomatoes**
½ cup **vegetable stock**
1 teaspoon **English mustard**
1 tablespoon **light brown
  sugar**
1 **green** or **red bell pepper**,
  cored, seeded, and diced
salt and **pepper**

To serve
4 **hamburger buns**
shredded lettuce

Preheat the slow cooker if necessary; see the manufacturer's instructions. Grease the inside of 2 x 12 fl oz soufflé dishes with a diameter of 4 inches and a height of 2½ inches with a little oil. Line the bottoms with nonstick parchment paper.

Add half the scallions, the beef, sausagemeat, and bread crumbs to a bowl or food processor. Add 1 tablespoon of the Worcestershire sauce, season with salt and pepper, and mix together. Divide between the 2 dishes and press down well to level off the surface. Cover with foil and put the dishes side by side in the slow-cooker pot.

Add the tomatoes, stock, remaining Worcestershire sauce, mustard, and sugar to a small saucepan. Season with salt and pepper and bring to a boil. Stir in the remaining scallions and the green or red bell pepper and spoon the mixture into the gaps around the dishes.

Cover with the lid and cook on high for 3 to 4 hours until the burgers are cooked. Test with a skewer to make sure the juices do not run pink. Lift the burger dishes out of the slow cooker with oven mitts, pour the excess fat out of the dishes, then turn the burgers out.

Split the hamburger buns and add lettuce to the bottom halves. Cut the burgers in half horizontally. Place 1 half on each bun, then top with spoonfuls of the tomato sauce and serve the remaining sauce in a small bowl. Accompany with oven-baked French fries, if liked.

For turkey burger & tomato sauce, omit the ground beef and add ½ lb ground turkey leg. Make and cook the recipe as above.

beef chile with cheesy tortillas

Preparation time **20 minutes**
Cooking temperature **low**
Cooking time **8 to 10 hours**
Serves **4**

1 tablespoon **sunflower oil**
1 lb **extra-lean ground beef**
1 **onion**, chopped
2 **garlic cloves**, minced
1 teaspoon **smoked paprika**
½ teaspoon **crushed red
    chile flakes**
1 teaspoon **ground cumin**
1 tablespoon **all-purpose
    flour**
14 oz can **diced tomatoes**
14 oz can **red kidney beans**,
    drained
½ cup **beef stock**
1 tablespoon **dark brown
    sugar**
salt and **pepper**

Topping
3½ oz **tortilla chips**
½ **red bell pepper**, cored,
    seeded, and diced
1 tablespoon freshly chopped
    cilantro
1 cup shredded **sharp
    Cheddar cheese**

Preheat the slow cooker if necessary; see the manufacturer's instructions. Heat the oil in a skillet, add the ground beef and onion, and fry, stirring constantly, for 5 minutes, breaking up the meat with a spoon, until it is browned.

Stir in the garlic, paprika, crushed chile flakes, and cumin and cook for 2 minutes. Stir in the flour. Mix in the tomatoes, kidney beans, stock, and sugar, season with salt and pepper, and pour the mixture into the slow-cooker pot. Cover with the lid and cook on low for 8 to 10 hours until the beef is tender.

Stir the chile, then arrange the tortilla chips on top. Sprinkle with the remaining topping ingredients, lift the pot out of the housing using oven mitts, and brown the chile under a preheated hot broiler until the cheese just melts. Spoon into bowls to serve.

For turkey fajitas with guacamole, make the chile as above using 1 lb ground turkey instead of the beef. To serve, halve, seed, and peel 1 avocado and mash the flesh with the juice of 1 lime, a small bunch of torn fresh cilantro, and some salt and pepper. Spoon the turkey mixture onto 8 warmed, medium-sized, soft flour tortillas, top with spoonfuls of the guacamole, dollop 1 tablespoon sour cream on each, and roll up to serve.

spiced lamb wraps

Preparation time **20 minutes**
Cooking temperature **low**
Cooking time **8 to 9 hours**
Serves **4**

1 tablespoon **olive oil**
1 lb **ground lamb**
1 **red onion**, finely chopped
2 teaspoons **ground cumin**
1 teaspoon **ground cinnamon**
½ teaspoon **chili powder**
1 teaspoon **dried oregano**
1 tablespoon **tomato paste**
½ cup **bulgur wheat**
2½ cups **boiling beef stock**
salt and **pepper**

To serve
8 large, **soft, flour wraps**
1¾ cups **hummus**
1 **romaine lettuce**, shredded
small handful of **mint**, finely
    chopped
½ **cucumber**, cut into strips

Preheat the slow cooker if necessary; see the manufacturer's instructions. Heat the oil in a skillet, add the ground lamb and onion, and fry for 5 minutes, stirring until the meat is evenly browned.

Stir in the ground spices, dried herbs, and tomato paste, then season with a little salt and pepper.

Spoon the mixture into the slow-cooker pot, add the bulgur wheat, then stir in the boiling stock. Cover with the lid and cook on low for 8 to 9 hours until the lamb is tender.

When ready to serve, warm the wraps in a dry skillet or in the microwave following the package instructions, then spread each one with a little hummus.

Stir the lamb mixture. Spoon it onto the wraps, then top with the lettuce, mint, and cucumber. Fold in the top and bottom of each wrap, then roll it up tightly to enclose the filling. Cut in half and serve immediately.

For beef & chile wraps, omit the lamb and fry 1 lb ground beef with the onion as above. Stir in the spices, herbs, and tomato paste as above, adding ¼ to ½ teaspoon crushed dried red chiles, to taste. Cook and serve as above.

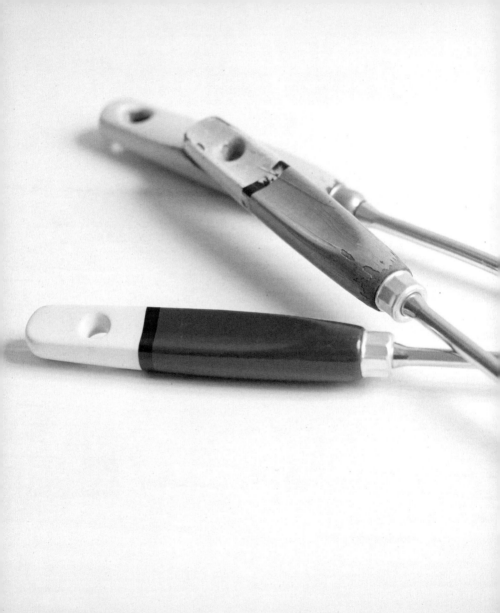

everyday
favorites

shallots baked with balsamic

Preparation time **20 minutes**
Cooking temperature **high**
Cooking time **4 to 5 hours**
Serves **4**

1 ½ lb **shallots**
½ stick **butter**, at room
   temperature
2 tablespoons **dark brown
   sugar**
2 tablespoons **balsamic
   vinegar**
2 tablespoons **sweet sherry**
   (optional)
leaves from 2 **rosemary
   sprigs**
salt and **pepper**

Preheat the slow cooker if necessary; see the manufacturer's instructions. Add the shallots to a large bowl, cover with boiling water, and let soak for 2 to 3 minutes to soften the skins.

Lift the shallots out of the water with a draining spoon, peel off the skins, and cut any large shallots in half.

Spread the butter all over the bottom of the slow cooker pot, add the shallots, then sprinkle them with the sugar and drizzle with the vinegar and sherry, if using. Scatter the rosemary leaves on top, season with salt and pepper, then cover with the lid.

Cook on high for 4 to 5 hours until tender, stirring the shallots once during cooking and again at the end. Serve with grilled sausages and mashed potatoes, if liked.

For shallot tarte tatin, transfer the shallots and cooking juices to an 8-inch skillet with an ovenproof handle or a solid cake pan (the type without a loose bottom). Roll out 8 oz puff pastry and trim to a circle a little larger than the skillet or cake pan. Place on top of shallots, tucking the pastry down into the inside edge. Prick the top 2 or 3 times, then place in a preheated oven, 400°F, for 30 minutes. Remove the pan from the oven and cover it with a large plate. Wearing oeven mitts, hold the two securely together and quickly flip them over. Set the plate on your work surface and lift the pan up off of the plate. Cut the tarte tatin into wedges to serve.

white beans with chipotle chile

Preparation time **20 minutes**
Cooking temperature **high**
Cooking time **4 to 5 hours**
Serves **4**

1 **dried chipotle chile**
3 tablespoons **boiling water**
2 tablespoons **olive oil**
1 **red onion**, coarsely chopped
2 **garlic cloves**, minced
½ teaspoon **ground cinnamon**
1 teaspoon **ground cumin**
1 teaspoon **dried oregano**
14 oz can **diced tomatoes**
1 cup **vegetable stock**
1 tablespoon **light brown sugar**
1 **sweet potato**, peeled and cut into ¾-inch cubes
1 **carrot**, diced
1 **red bell pepper**, cored, seeded, and diced
1¼ cups **cherry tomatoes**
14 oz can **cannellini beans**, drained
salt and **pepper**

Add the chile to a cup or small bowl, pour in the boiling water, and let stand for 15 minutes. Preheat the slow cooker if necessary; see the manufacturer's instructions. Heat the oil in a skillet, add the onion, and fry for 5 minutes, stirring constantly, until softened and just beginning to brown.

Stir in the garlic, spices, and herbs, then add the tomatoes, stock, and the sugar. Tip the chile-soaking water into the pan, then finely chop the chile and stir it in with salt and pepper. Bring to a boil, stirring.

Add the sweet potato, carrot, red bell pepper, and cherry tomatoes to the slow-cooker pot, then stir in the cannellini beans. Pour in the hot stock mixture and press the vegetables beneath the liquid as much as you can. Cover with the lid and cook on high for 4 to 5 hours until the vegetables are tender.

Stir again, then spoon into bowls and garnish with tortillas and cilantro leaves, if liked.

For beef and beans with chipotle chile, fry the onion with 1 lb ground beef. Make as above, omitting the white cannellini beans and sweet potato and adding a 14 oz can of drained red kidney beans instead. Cook on high for 4 to 5 hours.

quorn jalfrezi

Preparation time **20 minutes**
Cooking temperature **low**
Cooking time **4 to 5 hours**
Serves 4

1 **onion**, quartered
2 **garlic cloves**, halved
1 **green chile**, halved and
  seeded
1½-inch piece of **fresh ginger
  root**, peeled and sliced
handful of **cilantro**, plus extra
  to garnish (optional)
¼ cup **desiccated coconut**
2 tablespoons **sunflower oil**
1 teaspoon **ground coriander**
1 teaspoon **turmeric**
2 teaspoons **garam masala**
1 teaspoon **brown mustard
  seeds**
1¼ cup **vegetable stock**
11½ oz **Quorn pieces**
1¼ cups **cherry tomatoes**,
  halved
salt and **pepper**

To serve
rice
naan bread

Preheat the slow cooker if necessary; see the
manufacturer's instructions. Finely chop the onion,
garlic, chile, ginger, cilantro, and coconut together in a
food processor if you have one, or using a large knife.

Heat the oil in a skillet, add the onion mixture, and cook
over low heat for 2 to 3 minutes, stirring constantly, until
softened. Stir in the ground spices and mustard seeds,
cook for 1 minute, then mix in the stock, season with
salt and pepper, and bring to a boil.

Add the Quorn pieces and tomatoes to the slow-cooker
pot, then pour in the hot spice mixture. Cover with the lid
and cook on low for 4 to 5 hours until tender. Serve with
rice and naan bread, garnished with the extra cilantro
and coconut shavings, if liked.

For chicken jalfrezi, omit the Quorn pieces and add
1 lb boneless, skinless diced chicken thighs and the
tomatoes to the slow-cooker pot, pour in the hot spice
mixture, and cook as above for 8 to 9 hours until the
chicken is cooked through.

salmon & arugula tagliatelle

Preparation time **20 minutes**
Cooking temperature **low**
Cooking time **1¾ to 2¼ hours**
Serves **4**

4 **salmon fillets**, about
  1 lb 2 oz in total
1 **lemon**, sliced
2 small **bay leaves**, torn in half
1¼ cups **boiling fish stock**
1 lb **fresh tagliatelle**
8 oz **soft cheese with garlic
  and herbs**
4 oz bag **mixed salad, such
  as arugula, watercress,
  and spinach**
handful of **basil**, torn into
  pieces
salt and **black pepper**

Preheat the slow cooker if necessary; see the manufacturer's instructions. Arrange the salmon fillets so that they fit snugly in the bottom of the slow-cooker pot. Squeeze the juice from the lemon slices over the salmon, arrange the slices on top with the bay leaves, and season with a little salt and pepper.

Pour in the boiling stock, then cover and cook on low for 1¾ to 2¼ hours until the fish is cooked and breaks easily into evenly colored flakes when pressed with a knife.

When the salmon is ready, put the pasta into a large saucepan of boiling water. Cook for 3 minutes until just tender. Drain into a colander. Ladle 1 cup of the hot fish stock from the slow-cooker pot into the empty pasta pan, stir in the soft cheese, and heat until melted. Add the arugula and other leaves, heat for 2 minutes until just wilted, then stir in the pasta.

Remove the pan from the heat and lift the salmon out of the slow cooker. Remove the salmon skin, break the fish into large flakes, discarding any bones, and toss gently with the pasta and torn basil leaves.

Spoon into bowls and top with extra pepper and a little shredded Parmesan, if liked.

For smoked cod & arugula tagliatelle, set 1 lb 2 oz smoked cod into the bottom of the slow-cooker pot, add the bay leaves and boiling fish stock, omitting the lemon. Cook as above. Cook 1 cup frozen kernel corn with the pasta. Drain and continue as above, omitting the basil.

herb-crusted salmon with tomatoes

Preparation time **20 minutes**
Cooking temperature **high**
and **low**
Cooking time **1¼ to 1¾ hours**
Serves **4**

1 lb **mixed red** and **yellow cherry tomatoes** (or all red if preferred), halved
1 cup canned **diced tomatoes**
1 teaspoon **superfine sugar**
handful of **basil**, chopped
4 **salmon fillets**, weighing about 5 oz each
salt and **pepper**

Topping
2 tablespoons **olive oil**
¼ cup **fresh bread crumbs**
¼ cup freshly shredded **Parmesan cheese**

Preheat the slow cooker if necessary; see the manufacturer's instructions. Add the fresh and canned tomatoes to the slow-cooker pot, sprinkle with the sugar, and season with salt and pepper. Then scatter with a little of the chopped basil.

Arrange the salmon in a single layer on top, scatter with more chopped basil (reserving 2 tablespoons for the topping), and salt and pepper. Cover with the lid and cook on high for 1¼ hours or until the salmon is opaque and the fish breaks into evenly colored flakes when pressed with a knife. If you are not ready to serve, reduce to low for a further 30 minutes.

When ready to serve, heat the oil in a small skillet, add the bread crumbs and Parmesan, and fry, stirring constantly, over medium heat until golden brown and crispy. Stir in the reserved chopped basil.

Spoon the tomatoes into shallow serving dishes, place the fish on top, and then spoon the crumb topping evenly onto each portion. Serve with salad, if liked.

For prosciutto-wrapped cod with cherry tomatoes, add the tomatoes, sugar, seasoning, and basil to the slow-cooker pot. Wrap 1 slice of prosciutto or Parma ham each around 4 thick 5 oz pieces of cod. Arrange in the slow cooker in a single layer, scatter with basil, then cook and serve as above.

smoked mackerel kedgeree

Preparation time **15 minutes**
Cooking temperature **low**
Cooking time **3¼ to 4¼ hours**
Serves **4**

1 tablespoon **sunflower oil**
1 **onion**, chopped
1 teaspoon **turmeric**
2 tablespoons **mango chutney**
3¼ to 3¾ cups **vegetable stock**
1 **bay leaf**
1 cup **easy-cook brown rice**
3 **smoked mackerel fillets**, about 8 oz in total, skinned
¾ cup **frozen peas**
1½ cups **watercress** or **arugula leaves**
4 **hard-cooked eggs**, cut into wedges
salt and **pepper**

Preheat the slow cooker if necessary; see the manufacturer's instructions. Heat the oil in a skillet, add the onion, and fry, stirring constantly, for 5 minutes or until softened and just beginning to turn golden.

Stir in the turmeric, chutney, stock, bay leaf, and a little salt and pepper and bring to a boil. Pour the mixture into the slow-cooker pot and add the rice. Add the smoked mackerel to the pot in a single layer. Cover with the lid and cook on low for 3 to 4 hours or until the rice is tender and has absorbed almost all of the stock.

Mix in the peas. Break up the fish into chunky pieces. Add extra hot stock if needed to loosen the rice (it will have absorbed a lot of the cooking liquid by now), then re-cover and cook for 15 minutes more. Stir in the watercress or arugula, spoon onto plates, and garnish with wedges of hard-cooked egg.

For smoked haddock kedgeree with cardamom, make the recipe as above but omit the mango chutney and, instead, add 4 crushed cardamom pods with their black seeds. Replace the smoked mackerel with 14 oz skinned smoked haddock fillet, cut into 2 pieces. Continue as above, adding the peas and egg wedges at the end but omitting the arugula or watercress. Drizzle with ¼ cup heavy cream.

all-in-one chicken casserole

Preparation time **20 minutes**
Cooking temperature **low**
Cooking time **8¼ to**
 10¼ hours
Serves **4**

1 tablespoon **olive oil**
4 **chicken legs**, weighing
 1¾ lb in total
2 oz **smoked Canadian
 bacon**, trimmed of fat and
 chopped
10½ oz **baby new potatoes**,
 thickly sliced
2 **small leeks**, thickly sliced,
 white and green parts kept
 separate
2 **celery stalks**, thickly sliced
2 **carrots**, sliced
2 teaspoons **all-purpose flour**
1 teaspoon **dried mixed
 herbs**
1 teaspoon **mustard powder**
2 cups **chicken stock**
2 oz **curly kale**, sliced
salt and **pepper**

Put half the olive oil into a large skillet and set it over high heat. When the pan is hot, add the chicken and cook for 5 minutes, turning, until browned all over. Transfer to the slow-cooker pot.

Add the bacon and potatoes to the skillet with the remaining olive oil and cook for 4 to 5 minutes, stirring, until the bacon is beginning to brown. Stir in the white leek slices (reserving the green slices), the celery and carrots. Add the flour, herbs, and mustard and stir well.

Pour in the stock, season to taste, and bring to a boil, stirring. Spoon the mixture over the chicken, cover, and cook on low for 8 to 10 hours or until the chicken is thoroughly cooked and the meat juices run clear when the thickest parts of the leg are pierced with a sharp knife.

Add the reserved green leek slices and the kale to the slow-cooker pot, re-cover, and cook for 15 minutes until the vegetables are just tender. Serve in shallow bowls.

For chicken hotpot, follow the main recipe to make the chicken mixture, omitting the new potatoes and carrots. Transfer to the slow-cooker pot and cover with 10½ oz scrubbed and thinly sliced baking potatoes and 2 thinly sliced carrots, arranging the slices so that each piece overlaps the next. Dot with 1½ tablespoons butter and season to taste, then cook as above. After cooking, brown the top under the broiler, if liked.

piri piri chicken

Preparation time **20 minutes**,
  plus overnight marinating
Cooking temperature **low**
Cooking time **8 to 9 hours**
Serves **4**

1¼ lb **skinless, boneless
  chicken thighs**, cut
  into large chunks
2 tablespoons **olive oil**
2 tablespoons **red wine
  vinegar**
1 tablespoon **tomato paste**
1 tablespoon **light brown
  sugar**
2 teaspoons **piri piri
  spice blend**
1 **red onion**, finely chopped
2 **garlic cloves**, minced
1 **red bell pepper**, cored,
  seeded, and diced
1 **yellow bell pepper**, cored,
  seeded, and diced
14 oz can **diced tomatoes**
½ cup **chicken stock**
1 tablespoon **cornstarch**
salt and **pepper**
chopped **parsley**, to garnish

Put the chicken into a large, sturdy, resealable plastic
food bag. Mix the oil, vinegar, tomato paste, sugar, and
piri piri spice blend together in a bowl with a little salt
and pepper. Pour the mixture into the bag containing
the chicken, then add the onion, garlic, and bell peppers.
Seal the bag, then shake the contents together to mix.
Let marinate overnight in the refrigerator.

Preheat the slow cooker if necessary; see the
manufacturer's instructions. Add the tomatoes and stock
to a small saucepan. Mix the cornstarch to a paste with
a little cold water, add the paste to the pan, and bring
the mixture to a boil, stirring.

Add the contents of the food bag to the slow-cooker
pot, pour in the hot tomato mixture, then cover and
cook on low for 8 to 9 hours until the chicken is cooked
through. Stir well, then scatter with the parsley and
serve with rice, if liked.

For piri piri vegetables, omit the chicken and chicken
stock. Add ¾ lb white mushrooms, halved, and a
14 oz can drained cannellini beans to the marinade
in the bag. Seal and chill overnight, or cook immediately,
if preferred. Continue and cook as above.

sweet & sour chicken

Preparation time **20 minutes**
Cooking temperature **low**
Cooking time **7¼ to 8½ hours**
Serves **4**

1 tablespoon **sunflower oil**
2 lb **skinless, boneless chicken thighs**, cubed
4 **scallions**, thickly sliced, white and green parts kept separate
2 **carrots**, halved lengthwise and thinly sliced
1 inch piece of **fresh ginger root**, finely chopped
14 oz can **pineapple chunks in juice**
1¼ cups **chicken stock**
1 tablespoon **cornstarch**
1 tablespoon **tomato paste**
2 tablespoons **superfine sugar**
2 tablespoons **soy sauce**
2 tablespoons **malt vinegar**
7½ oz can **bamboo shoots**, drained
1¼ cups **bean sprouts**
1 cup **snow peas**, thinly sliced

Preheat the slow cooker if necessary; see the manufacturer's instructions. Heat the oil in a large skillet over high heat, add the chicken, and cook for 3 to 4 minutes until browned on all sides. Add the white scallion slices (reserving the green slices), the carrots, and ginger and cook for 2 minutes.

Stir in the pineapple chunks with their juice and the stock. Put the cornstarch, tomato paste, and sugar in a small bowl, then mix in the soy sauce and vinegar to make a smooth paste. Add to the pan and bring to a boil, stirring.

Transfer the mixture to the slow-cooker pot, add the bamboo shoots, and press the chicken pieces into the liquid. Cover and cook on low for 7 to 8 hours until the chicken is cooked through.

Add the reserved green scallion slices, the bean sprouts, and snow peas, and mix well. Re-cover and cook for 15 minutes or until the vegetables are just tender. Serve with boiled rice, if liked.

For sweet & sour chicken with chile, make the recipe as above, adding 1 seeded and chopped mild red chile along with the pineapple. Serve with a little bowl of extra chopped chile to scatter when serving, if liked.

paprika pork & cornmeal dumplings

Preparation time **25 minutes**
Cooking temperature **low**
and **high**
Cooking time **9 to 10 hours**
Serves **4**

3 tablespoons **olive oil**
1 ½ lb **boneless pork
shoulder**, cubed
2 **red onions**, cubed
½ to 1 teaspoon **hot smoked
paprika** (to taste)
½ teaspoon **ground cumin**
½ teaspoon **ground cinnamon**
14 oz can **baked beans**
14 oz can **diced tomatoes**
1 cup **beef stock**
10½ oz **chantenay carrots**,
larger ones halved
salt and **pepper**

Dumplings
½ cup **fine cornmeal**
½ cup **all-purpose flour**
sifted with 1 teaspoon
baking powder
2 **scallions**, chopped
1 cup shredded **Cheddar
cheese**
2 **eggs**
½ cup **plain yogurt**

Preheat the slow cooker if necessary; see the manufacturer's instructions. Heat 1 tablespoon of the olive oil in a saucepan, then add the pork, a few pieces at a time, until all the pieces are in the pan. Fry for 5 minutes until the meat is just beginning to brown, then stir in the onions and cook for a few minutes until they just begin to soften.

Stir in the paprika, cumin, and cinnamon, then mix in the baked beans, tomatoes, and stock. Season with salt and pepper, then bring to a boil, stirring constantly.

Spoon into the slow-cooker pot, add the carrots, and press the carrots and pork beneath the liquid. Cover with the lid and cook on low for 8 to 9 hours until the meat and carrots are tender.

Make the dumplings. Put the cornmeal and the flour and baking powder in a bowl. Stir in the scallions, cheese, and a little salt and pepper. Add the eggs, yogurt, and remaining olive oil and lightly beat.

Take the lid off the stew, drop spoonfuls of the dumpling mixture over the top, leaving a little space between the spoonfuls if you can. Re-cover with the lid and cook on high for 1 hour until the dumplings are well risen and firm. Take the slow-cooker pot out of the machine with oven mitts and brown the top under a preheated broiler, if liked. Spoon into shallow bowls and serve with broccoli, if liked.

For paprika beef & wholegrain mustard cornmeal dumplings, fry 1 ½ lb cubed beef chuck in place of the pork, then continue as above. When making the dumplings, add 2 teaspoons wholegrain mustard along with the eggs, yogurt, and oil. Serve as above.

braised ham & leeks

Preparation time **20 minutes**
Cooking temperature **high**
Cooking time **5¼ to 6¼ hours**
Serves **4**

1½ lb **smoked ham,** well
    rinsed with cold water
2 **leeks**, thickly sliced,
    white and green parts
    kept separate
10½ oz **baby new potatoes**,
    scrubbed and larger ones
    halved
10½ oz **chantenay carrots**,
    larger ones halved
1 quart **dry apple cider** or
    chicken stock
1 teaspoon **Dijon mustard**
1 **chicken stock cube**,
    crumbled (omit this if using
    chicken stock in place of the
    dry apple cider)
2 **bay leaves**
4 **cloves**
1½ tablespoons **cornstarch**
pepper
handful of **parsley**, chopped,
    to garnish

Preheat the slow cooker if necessary; see the manufacturer's instructions. Place the ham in the center of the slow-cooker pot. Arrange the white leek slices (reserving the green slices), potatoes, and carrots around the ham.

Add the dry cider or stock, mustard, stock cube, bay leaves, and cloves to a saucepan. Season with pepper (don't add salt since the ham may be salty; better to taste and add at the end) and bring to a boil.

Pour the cider mixture into the slow-cooker pot, cover with the lid, and cook on high for 5 to 6 hours or until the ham is very tender.

Mix the cornstarch to a paste with a little water. Stir the paste into the cider sauce, then add the reserved green leek slices. Re-cover and cook for 15 minutes until the green leek slices are tender and the sauce has thickened slightly.

Lift the ham out of the slow cooker and cut it into thick, coarse shreds. Ladle the vegetables and sauce into shallow bowls, add some ham shreds, and scatter with the parsley.

For leek & ham with parsley sauce, omit the cider or chicken stock and cornstarch and add 1 quart vegetable stock. When the ham is cooked, pour off and reserve 1¼ cups of the hot stock. Melt ½ stick butter in a saucepan, stir in ½ cup all-purpose flour, then mix in the reserved stock and heat, stirring. Stir in 1¼ cups milk and a large handful of parsley, finely chopped. Cook until thickened. Season. Arrange the ham and vegetables on serving plates and serve with the sauce.

balsamic pork with red onions

Preparation time **20 minutes**
Cooking temperature **low**
Cooking time **8 to 9 hours**
Serves **4**

2 tablespoons **olive oil**
1¾ lb **boneless pork
   shoulder**, cut into chunks
1 **red onion**, cut into wedges
2 tablespoons **all-purpose
   flour**
2 cups **pork** or **chicken stock**
2 tablespoons **balsamic
   vinegar**
1 tablespoon **light brown
   sugar**
1 teaspoon **English mustard**
2¼ cups peeled **parsnip**
   chunks
1 **apple**, cored and diced
   (no need to peel)
salt and **pepper**
chopped **parsley**, to garnish

Preheat the slow cooker if necessary; see the manufacturer's instructions. Heat the oil in a large skillet, add the pork, and fry, stirring, until the meat is evenly browned. Scoop the chunks of pork out of the pan with a slotted spoon and add them to the slow-cooker pot. Add the onion to the skillet and fry for 5 minutes until softened.

Stir in the flour, then mix in the stock, and then the vinegar, sugar, and mustard. Season with salt and pepper. Bring to a boil, stirring. Add the parsnip chunks and diced apple to the slow-cooker pot, pour in the onion and stock mixture, and press the parsnips beneath the liquid, if needed. Cover and cook on low for 8 to 9 hours until the pork and parsnips are tender.

Sprinkle with chopped parsley and serve spooned into shallow bowls.

For cider-braised pork with red onions & parsnips, make the recipe as above, omitting the balsamic vinegar and using 1 cup dry apple cider and 1 cup pork or chicken stock for the cooking liquid.

beef adobo

Preparation time **25 minutes**
Cooking temperature **low**
Cooking time **8 to 10 hours**
Serves **4**

1 tablespoon **sunflower oil**
1½ lb **beef chuck**, fat
  discarded, cubed
1 large **onion**, sliced
2 **garlic cloves**, minced
2 tablespoons **all-purpose
  flour**
2 cups **beef stock**
¼ cup **soy sauce**
¼ cup **white wine vinegar**
1 tablespoon **superfine sugar**
2 **bay leaves**
juice of 1 **lime**
salt and **pepper**
rice, to serve

To garnish
1 **carrot**, cut into thin sticks
½ bunch of **scallions**,
  cut into shreds
cilantro leaves

Preheat the slow cooker if necessary; see the manufacturer's instructions. Heat the oil in a large skillet over high heat and add the beef, a few pieces at a time, until all the meat has been added. Fry, turning the beef, until evenly browned, then lift out of the pan with a slotted spoon and transfer to a plate.

Put the onion into the skillet and fry for 5 minutes or until it is just beginning to brown. Mix in the garlic and cook for 2 minutes. Stir in the flour, then gradually mix in the stock. Add the soy sauce, vinegar, sugar, bay leaves, and salt and pepper and bring to a boil, stirring.

Transfer the beef to the slow-cooker pot, pour in the onion and stock mixture, cover with the lid, and cook on low for 8 to 10 hours until the beef is tender.

Stir in lime juice to taste. Serve in shallow bowls lined with rice. Garnish with carrot sticks, shredded scallions, and cilantro leaves.

For hoisin beef, combine 3 tablespoons each of soy sauce and rice or wine vinegar with 2 tablespoons hoisin sauce and a 1-inch piece of peeled and finely chopped fresh ginger root. Add this mixture to the beef stock with the sugar. Omit the bay leaves. Bring the mixture to a boil, then continue as above, adding the lime juice just before serving.

beef lasagne

Preparation time **25 minutes**
Cooking temperature **low**
Cooking time **5 to 6¼ hours**
Serves 4

1 tablespoon **olive oil**
1 lb **ground beef**
1 **onion**, chopped
1 **red bell pepper**, cored,
    seeded, and diced
1 **green bell pepper**, cored,
    seeded, and diced
2 cups **button mushrooms**,
    sliced
2 **celery stalks**, chopped
2 **garlic cloves**, minced
2 cups **tomato puree**
1 cup **beef stock**
½ cup **red wine** or **extra beef
    stock**, if preferred
1 teaspoon **dried oregano**
4 oz **dried lasagne noodles**
salt and **pepper**

Topping
8 oz **mascarpone cheese**
2 **eggs**
¼ cup freshly shredded
    Parmesan cheese

Preheat the slow cooker if necessary; see the manufacturer's instructions. Heat the oil in a large skillet, add the ground beef and onion, and fry, covered, for 10 minutes, stirring from time to time, until browned.

Add the bell peppers, mushrooms, celery, and garlic and fry for a further 5 minutes, stirring more frequently.

Mix in the tomato puree, stock, and wine, if using, then the dried herbs, and season with salt and pepper to taste. Bring to a boil, stirring.

Spoon one-quarter of the beef mixture into the bottom of the slow-cooker pot. Cover with one-third of the lasagne noodles, breaking them into large pieces so that they fit in a single layer. Continue layering in this way, ending with a layer of ground beef.

Cover with the lid and cook on low for 4 to 5 hours until the beef and vegetables are tender. Beat the mascarpone, eggs, and a little salt and pepper together until smooth. Spoon the mixture over the top of the lasagne, spreading it out into an even layer. Scatter with the Parmesan, then re-cover and cook for 1 to 1¼ hours or until the topping is just set.

Lift the slow-cooker pot out of the machine with oven mitts, then brown the lasagne under a preheated broiler. Spoon into shallow bowls and serve with salad, if liked.

For beef moussaka, make the meat mixture as above, omitting the lasagne noodles and layering with 2 sliced and fried eggplants. Cook on low as above, then top with the mascarpone topping and cook until set. Broil, if liked, then serve as above.

easy lamb & barley risotto

Preparation time **10 minutes**
Cooking temperature **low**
Cooking time **7 to 8 hours**
Serves **4**

¾ oz **mixed dried
  mushrooms**
1 quart **boiling vegetable
  stock**
¼ cup **sweet sherry** or **fresh
  orange juice**
1 **onion**, finely chopped
1 teaspoon **ground cumin**
2 **garlic cloves**, minced
¼ cup **golden raisins**
¾ cup **pearl barley**
4 **lamb chops**, about
  5 oz each
2½ cups **ready-prepared
  pumpkin** or **butternut
  squash**, cut into
  ¾-inch cubes
salt and **pepper**
chopped **mint** and **parsley**,
  to garnish

Preheat the slow cooker if necessary; see the
manufacturer's instructions. Add the dried mushrooms
to the slow-cooker pot, pour in the boiling stock, then
stir in the sherry or orange juice, onion, cumin, garlic,
and golden raisins. Spoon in the barley and season
with salt and pepper.

Arrange the chops on top in a single layer, season,
then tuck the pumpkin or squash into the gaps between
the chops. Press the chops and squash down lightly into
the stock, then cover with the lid and cook on low for
7 to 8 hours until the lamb and vegetables are tender.

Lift the chops out of the slow cooker, stir the barley,
then spoon onto plates. Top with the chops, broken into
pieces, and scatter with the herbs. Serve with spoonfuls
of harissa, if liked.

For pumpkin & barley risotto, omit the lamb and use
3½ cups diced pumpkin. Cook as above, then add 4 oz
spinach to the risotto for the last 15 minutes of cooking.
Serve topped with spoonfuls of Greek yogurt, chopped
fresh mint and parsley, and buttery fried sliced almonds.

pot roast lamb with za'atar rub

Preparation time **20 minutes**
Cooking temperature **high**
Cooking time **5 to 6 hours**
Serves **4**

1 tablespoon **extra virgin olive oil**
2 **onions**, thinly sliced
2 **garlic cloves**, minced
1 cup **lamb stock**
1 tablespoon **tomato paste**
2 teaspoons **za'atar spice mix**, divided
1 cup **dry white wine** or extra **lamb stock**, if preferred
1 tablespoon **cornstarch**
¾ lb **new potatoes**, scrubbed and thickly sliced
½ **boneless lamb shoulder**, weighing about 1 ½ lb
salt and **pepper**
chopped **parsley** and **mint**, to garnish

To serve
2 **zucchini**, thinly sliced
1 tablespoon **olive oil**
½ teaspoon **za'atar spice mix**
1¾ cups **hummus**

Preheat the slow cooker if necessary; see the manufacturer's instructions. Heat the oil in a large skillet, add the onions, and fry for 5 minutes until softened and just beginning to brown. Stir in the garlic, stock, tomato paste, and half the za'atar. Pour in the wine, if using, reserving about 2 tablespoons of wine or stock.

Stir the cornstarch into the reserved wine or stock until smooth, then add to the skillet. Bring to a boil, stirring.

Add the potatoes to the bottom of the slow-cooker pot, then pour in the hot stock mixture. Remove the butcher's strings from the lamb and open it out flat. Rub with the remaining za'atar and season with salt and pepper. Add to the slow-cooker pot and press the meat beneath the liquid. Cover with the lid and cook on high for 5 to 6 hours or until the lamb is almost falling apart.

Toss the sliced zucchini with the oil, za'atar, and a little salt and pepper. Cook on a preheated ridged grill pan until lightly browned and tender. Divide the hummus among 4 plates, spread into an even layer, and make a thin ridge around the sides to contain the lamb sauce. Break the lamb into pieces, then spoon it onto the hummus, along with the sauce. Add the zucchini and scatter with chopped parsley and mint.

For pot roast lamb with rosemary, add 1 cup red wine in place of the white wine, if using, in the sauce, plus 2 tablespoons redcurrant jelly and 3 sprigs of fresh rosemary. Mix the cornstarch with the reserved wine or stock as above. Add the potatoes and plain bone-in lamb roast to the slow cooker, then add the hot stock mixture. Cook as above and serve with mixed steamed vegetables.

easy
shortcuts

salmon tikka salad

Preparation time **20 minutes**
Cooking temperature **low**
Cooking time **1¾ to 2 hours**
Serves **4**

4 **salmon fillets**, about
   4 oz each
1 tablespoon **tikka masala
   curry paste**
small handful of **cilantro**,
   coarsely chopped
juice of 1 **lemon**
½ cup **boiling fish stock**
salt and **pepper**

To serve
2 **Little Gem lettuces**
small handful of **cilantro**
½ **cucumber,** thinly sliced
1 cup thinly sliced, trimmed
   radishes
½ cup **plain yogurt**
½ **red onion**, thinly sliced

Preheat the slow cooker if necessary; see the manufacturer's instructions. Arrange the salmon in a single layer in the bottom of the slow-cooker pot. Spread the top of the salmon with the curry paste, then scatter with the chopped cilantro and sprinkle with the lemon juice.

Pour in the boiling stock, season with a little salt and pepper, then cover with the lid. Cook on low for 1¾ to 2 hours or until the salmon is cooked through and flakes easily.

When the salmon is ready, thickly slice the lettuce and arrange on serving plates with a few cilantro leaves. Finely chop the remaining cilantro and place it in a bowl with the cucumber, radishes, and yogurt. Season with salt and pepper and toss together. Spoon the mixture onto the lettuce.

Lift the salmon out of the slow cooker with a slotted spoon, break into pieces, discarding any skin and bones, and spoon onto the salad. Scatter with the red onion slices and serve immediately.

For harissa salmon salad, spread the salmon with 1 tablespoon harissa paste, then cook and serve as above.

mexican baked beans

Preparation time **15 minutes**
Cooking temperature **low**
Cooking time **8 to 9 hours**
Serves **4**

2 cups mixed **ready-diced
carrots and turnips**
2 x 10½ oz cans **hot and
spicy mixed beans**
1 lb **tomatoes**, skinned, if
liked, coarsely chopped
2 **garlic cloves**, minced
(optional)
1 teaspoon **dried oregano**
8 large **soft tortilla wraps**,
to serve

Preheat the slow cooker if necessary; see the manufacturer's instructions. Add the diced carrots and turnips to the bottom of the slow-cooker pot. Pour in the canned beans and their sauce, add the tomatoes, garlic, if using, and the oregano and stir together.

Cover with the lid and cook on low for 8 to 9 hours until the vegetables are tender.

When ready to serve, warm the tortillas following the package instructions. Spoon the spicy beans into bowls and serve with tortillas and dollops of sour cream and shredded cheese, if liked.

For Mexican baked beans & smoked ham, trim the fat from 1 large ham steak and dice the steak, then add the ham to the slow cooker with the other ingredients. Cook and serve as above.

green bean risotto with pesto

Preparation time **20 minutes**
Cooking temperature **low**
Cooking time **2 hours**
5 minutes to 2½ hours
Serves **4**

2 tablespoons **butter**
1 tablespoon **olive oil**
1 **onion**, chopped
2 **garlic cloves**, chopped
1¼ cups **risotto rice**
1¼ quarts **boiling vegetable
    stock,** divided
2 teaspoons **pesto**
4 oz **frozen extra fine green
    snap beans**
1 cup **frozen peas**
salt and **pepper**

To garnish
Parmesan shavings
basil leaves

Preheat the slow cooker if necessary; see the manufacturer's instructions. Heat the butter and oil in a saucepan, add the onion, and fry, stirring constantly, for 5 minutes until softened and just starting to brown.

Stir in the garlic and rice and cook for 1 minute. Add all but ½ cup of the stock, season with salt and pepper, then bring to a boil. Transfer to the slow-cooker pot, cover with the lid, and cook on low for 1¾ to 2 hours until the rice is tender.

Stir in the pesto and the remaining stock if more liquid is needed. Place the frozen vegetables on top of the rice, re-cover, and cook for a further 20 to 30 minutes or until the vegetables are cooked through. Serve garnished with Parmesan shavings and basil leaves.

For green bean risotto with sage & pancetta, add 3 oz diced pancetta or smoked bacon when frying the chopped onion. Add 2 sprigs of sage to the mixture when adding the stock instead of the pesto. Replace the basil leaves with some small sage leaves.

mixed vegetable balti

Preparation time **20 minutes**
Cooking temperature **low**
Cooking time **5 to 6 hours**
Serves **4**

1 small **cauliflower**, cut
 into florets
2¾ cups cubed **sweet potato**,
 cut into ¾-inch pieces
1 **red pepper**, cored, seeded,
 and cut into chunks
3½ oz **green snap beans**,
 each cut into 3
2 cups ready-made **balti
 sauce**

To serve
1 tablespoon **olive oil**
1 **onion**, thinly sliced
handful of chopped **cilantro
 leaves**
1 teaspoon **brown mustard
 seeds**
½ cup **Greek yogurt**
naan bread

Preheat the slow cooker if necessary; see the manufacturer's instructions. Add the cauliflower, sweet potato, red bell pepper, and green snap beans to the slow-cooker pot.

Pour the curry sauce into a saucepan and bring to a boil, or microwave, if preferred. Pour the sauce onto the vegetables, cover, and cook on low for 5 to 6 hours or until the vegetables are just tender. Stir halfway through the cooking time and again at the end.

When ready to serve, heat the oil in a skillet, add the onion and chopped cilantro, and fry for 4 to 5 minutes until softened and browned. Stir in the mustard seeds and cook for a further 1 to 2 minutes more.

Spoon the curry into bowls and top with spoonfuls of the yogurt and the fried onion mixture. Serve with warmed naan bread.

For chicken & vegetable balti, omit the cauliflower and replace with 1¼ lb skinless, boneless, diced chicken thighs. Add the remaining vegetables and hot sauce and cook on low for 8 to 9 hours until the chicken is cooked through and the vegetables are tender. Serve as above.

red bell pepper & chorizo tortilla

Preparation time **20 minutes**
Cooking temperature **high**
Cooking time **2 to 2½ hours**
Serves **4**

1 tablespoon **olive oil**, plus
extra for greasing
1 small **onion**, chopped
3 oz **chorizo sausage**, diced
6 **eggs**
½ cup **milk**
3½ oz **roasted red bell
peppers from a jar**, sliced
½ lb **potatoes**, cooked and
sliced
salt and **pepper**

Preheat the slow cooker if necessary. Lightly oil a
1½ quart ovenproof soufflé dish and line the bottom
with nonstick parchment paper. Heat the oil in a small
skillet over medium heat, add the onion and chorizo, and
cook for 4 to 5 minutes until the onion has softened.

Beat the eggs and milk together in a mixing bowl and
season to taste. Add the onion and chorizo, red bell
peppers, and potatoes and toss together.

Tip the mixture into the oiled dish, cover the top with
foil, and put in the slow-cooker pot. Pour boiling water
into the slow-cooker pot to come halfway up the sides
of the dish, cover, and cook on high for 2 to 2½ hours
until the egg mixture has just set in the center.

Loosen the edges of the tortilla with a metal spatula,
invert it onto a plate, and peel off the lining paper. Cut
into slices and serve hot or cold with salad, if liked.

For cheesy bacon & rosemary tortilla, follow the
recipe above, using 3 oz diced smoked bacon instead
of the chorizo. Beat the eggs and milk in a bowl with
the chopped leaves from 2 small rosemary sprigs,
¼ cup freshly shredded Parmesan or Cheddar cheese
and 1 cup sliced button mushrooms. Season to taste
and continue as above.

pork with black bean sauce

Preparation time **20 minutes**,
   plus overnight marinating
Cooking temperature **high**
   and **low**
Cooking time **8 to 10 hours**
Serves **4**

4 **pork rib chops**, about
   6 oz each
2 tablespoons **cornstarch**
¼ cup **soy sauce**
1½-inch piece of **fresh ginger
   root**, peeled and finely
   chopped
2 **garlic cloves**, minced
¼ cup **black bean sauce**
1¼ cups **boiling chicken
   stock**
chopped **cilantro leaves**,
   to garnish
pepper

To serve
1 tablespoon **sunflower oil**
10½ oz **mixed vegetables
   for stir-frying**
rice

Put the pork rib chops into a shallow nonmetallic dish.
Put the cornstarch and soy sauce in a small bowl and
mix to a smooth paste, then add the ginger, garlic, black
bean sauce, and a little pepper. Pour the mixture over
the pork, cover with plastic wrap, and marinate in the
refrigerator overnight.

Preheat the slow cooker if necessary; see the
manufacturer's instructions. Put the pork and marinade
into the slow-cooker pot. Pour in the boiling stock, cover
with the lid, and cook on high for 30 minutes. Reduce
the heat and cook on low for 7½ to 9½ hours or set to
auto for 8 to 10 hours until the pork is tender.

When almost ready to serve, heat the oil in a large
skillet, add the mixed vegetables, and stir-fry for 2 to
3 minutes or until just tender. Spoon the pork onto
plates lined with rice and top with the vegetables.

For sweet & sour pork, omit the black bean sauce
from the marinade, add the marinated pork to the slow-
cooker pot with 1 bunch of sliced scallions, 1 cored,
seeded, and sliced red bell pepper, and 1½ cups sliced
mushrooms. Replace the chicken stock with a 1¾ cups
ready-made sweet and sour sauce. Bring the sauce to
a boil in a saucepan or the microwave, then pour it into
the slow-cooker pot. Continue as above.

cheat's fish pie

Preparation time **20 minutes**
Cooking temperature **low**
Cooking time **2½ to 3 hours**
Serves **4**

1 ¼ lb **cubed fish-pie mix**
   (with salmon, white fish, and
   smoked fish)
4 **scallions**, thinly sliced
1 lb chilled carton ready-made
   cheese sauce
few drops of **Tabasco sauce**
1 ¾ cups **frozen peas**
1 lb chilled package **buttery
   mashed potatoes**
½ cup shredded **sharp
   Cheddar cheese**

Preheat the slow cooker if necessary; see manufacturer's instructions. Add the cubed fish to the bottom of the slow-cooker pot, then add the scallions, cheese sauce, and a few drops of Tabasco. Gently stir together. Level the surface, pressing the fish beneath the sauce.

Cover and cook on low for 2½ to 3 hours or until the fish is cooked and the sauce is piping hot.

When the fish is cooked, add the peas to a saucepan of boiling water, cook for 3 to 4 minutes, then drain and mash them. Heat the mashed potatoes in the microwave following to the package instructions, then stir in the peas.

Spoon the fish mixture into a large baking dish, spoon the mashed potatoes on top, then scatter with the shredded cheese. Cook under a preheated medium broiler until browned. Serve immediately.

For cheat's baked fish & pasta, cook the fish in the sauce as above. Cook 7 oz dried pasta twists in a saucepan of boiling water for 5 minutes, then add the frozen peas and cook for 4 to 5 minutes until the peas are hot and the pasta is tender. Drain, then stir into the sauce and spoon into a large shallow baking dish. Scatter with the shredded Cheddar cheese and 2 tablespoons fresh bread crumbs. Broil for 5 minutes until the top is crisp and golden.

peasant paella

Preparation time **20 minutes**
Cooking temperature **high**
Cooking time **4¾ to 6 hours**
Serves **4**

1 tablespoon **olive oil**
1 lb **skinless, boneless chicken thighs**, cubed
1 **onion**, chopped
2¼ oz **chorizo sausage**, sliced
2 **garlic cloves**, minced
1 **red bell pepper**, cored, seeded, and diced
1 **orange bell pepper**, cored, seeded, and diced
2 **celery stalks**, diced
2 pinches of **saffron threads**
½ teaspoon **dried Mediterranean herbs**
3¼ cups **boiling chicken stock**
1 cup **long-grain brown rice**
1 cup **frozen peas**
salt and **pepper**
2 tablespoons chopped **parsley**, to garnish

Preheat the slow cooker if necessary; see the manufacturer's instructions. Heat the oil in a large skillet over high heat until hot. Add the chicken, a few pieces at a time, until all the chicken is in the pan, then cook for 5 minutes, stirring, until browned. Use a slotted spoon to transfer the chicken to the slow-cooker pot.

Add the onion, chorizo, and garlic to the skillet and cook for 3 to 4 minutes, stirring, until the onion begins to color. Add the bell peppers and celery, stir well, then transfer to the slow-cooker pot. Mix the saffron and dried herbs with the boiling stock, season to taste, then pour into the slow-cooker pot and stir well. Cover and cook on high for 3 to 4 hours.

Place the rice in a sieve and rinse under cold running water, then stir into the chicken mixture. Re-cover and cook for 1½ to 1¾ hours until the rice is tender and the chicken is cooked through. Stir in the peas and continue cooking for 15 minutes. Serve garnished with chopped parsley.

For seafood paella, follow the recipe, omitting the chicken. Defrost a 13 oz package of frozen mixed seafood and pat it dry using paper towels. Heat 1 tablespoon olive oil in a large skillet, add the seafood, and fry for 4 to 5 minutes until it is piping hot. Stir into the finished paella and garnish with the parsley.

chinese lemon chicken

Preparation time **15 minutes**
Cooking temperature **low**
Cooking time **8 to 9 hours**
Serves **4**

1¼ lb **skinless, boneless chicken thighs**, cubed
4 **scallions**, sliced
2 cups ready-made **Peking lemon sauce**
1 tablespoon **sunflower oil**
10½ oz package **oriental stir-fry vegetables with sliced bamboo shoots and water chestnuts**
juice of 1 **lemon**
rice, to serve

Preheat the slow cooker if necessary; see the manufacturer's instructions. Add the chicken and scallions to the slow-cooker pot.

Bring the sauce to a boil in a saucepan or in a bowl in the microwave. Pour the sauce over the chicken in the slow-cooker pot, then cover with the lid and cook on low for 8 to 9 hours until the chicken is cooked through.

When ready to serve, heat the oil in a skillet, add the stir-fry vegetables, and cook for 2 to 3 minutes until piping hot. Stir the lemon juice into the chicken, then spoon it into rice-lined bowls and top with the stir-fried vegetables. Garnish with lemon zest curls, if liked.

For Chinese lemon salmon, add 4 salmon pieces, about 4 oz each, to the bottom of the slow-cooker pot with the scallions instead of the chicken. Continue as the recipe above, but cook on low for 1½ to 1¾ hours, then top with the stir-fried vegetables.

chicken ratatouille

Preparation time **15 minutes**
Cooking temperature **low**
Cooking time **8 to 9 hours**
Serves **4**

1 ¼ lb **skinless, boneless chicken thighs**, halved
4 strips **smoked bacon**, diced
1 lb package **frozen chargrilled Mediterranean vegetables**
¾ cup canned **diced tomatoes**
1 ¼ cups **water**
1 ½ oz sachet **powdered chicken in red wine sauce for slow cookers**
2 **garlic cloves**, minced
basil leaves, to garnish

Preheat the slow cooker if necessary; see the manufacturer's instructions. Add the chicken and bacon to the slow-cooker pot, then scatter the frozen vegetables on top.

Add the tomatoes, measurement water, sauce mixture, and garlic to a saucepan and bring to a boil, stirring until smooth. Pour the mixture evenly over the chicken and bacon, then cover with the lid and cook on low for 8 to 9 hours until the chicken is cooked through.

Garnish with basil leaves and serve with flatbread, if liked.

For spicy sausage ratatouille, omit the chicken and add 10½ oz Kabanos polish sausage, thickly sliced, to the slow-cooker pot with the bacon and remaining ingredients. Cook as above.

turkey, leek & cranberry pies

Preparation time **25 minutes**,
plus **20 minutes** in a
conventional oven
Cooking temperature **low**
Cooking time **8 to 9 hours**
Serves **4**

1 lb **turkey breast slices**,
cubed
1 **leek**, thinly sliced
2 cups **button mushrooms**,
sliced
14 oz can **red wine cooking
sauce** or **tomato-based
pasta sauce**
½ cup **water**
juice of ½ **orange**
2 tablespoons **cranberry
sauce**
11 oz **chilled ready-rolled,
all-butter puff pastry**
beaten egg, to glaze

Preheat the slow cooker if necessary; see the
manufacturer's instructions. Add the turkey, leek,
and mushrooms to the slow-cooker pot.

Pour the cooking sauce, measurement water, and
orange juice into a saucepan and add the cranberry
sauce. Bring to a boil, stirring. Alternatively, heat the
mixture in a microwave. Pour the liquid into the slow-
cooker pot, press the turkey beneath the surface of
the sauce, then cover with the lid and cook on low
for 8 to 9 hours until the turkey is cooked through.

Spoon the turkey mixture into 4 individual round pie
dishes or ramekins with a diameter of 4½ inches and
depth of 2½ inches. Unroll the pastry, cut out 4 round
pastry lids, using the dishes as a size guide, and stick
1 lid onto the rim of each dish using a little beaten egg
to cover the turkey mixture. Brush the pastry tops with
beaten egg and decorate with shapes cut out from
any pastry scraps or trimmings.

Bake in a preheated oven, 400°F, for 15 to 20 minutes
until the pastry is puffed and golden. Serve with broccoli
and green beans, if liked.

For garlicky lamb, leek & cranberry pies, omit
the turkey and replace with 1¼ lb ground lamb and
2 minced garlic cloves. Add the remaining ingredients
and cook and serve as above.

beef & ale stew with herb dumplings

Preparation time **20 minutes**

Cooking temperature **low and high**

Cooking time **8½ to 9 hours 40 minutes**

Serves **4**

1½ lb **lean beef chuck**, cubed

1 cup each ready-diced **carrots and turnips**

1 **leek**, thickly sliced

2 **portobello mushrooms**, sliced

2 cups ready-made **beef and ale cooking sauce** or **beef soup**

½ cup **beef stock**

4½ oz package **herb-flavored dumpling mix**

small handful of **parsley**, finely chopped

Preheat the slow cooker if necessary; see manufacturer's instructions. Add the beef to the slow-cooker pot, scatter with the diced carrots and turnips, and the leek and mushrooms, then mix together.

Pour the sauce and stock into a saucepan, bring to a boil, stirring, then pour the mixture evenly over the meat in the slow-cooker pot. Press the raw ingredients beneath the surface of the liquid. Cover with the lid and cook on low for 8 to 9 hours until the beef is tender.

Make the dumplings. Mix the dumpling mix with cold water and chopped parsley following the package instructions to make a soft dough. Cut the dough into 12 equal pieces and shape them into small balls.

Stir the casserole, place the dumplings on top in a single layer, leaving small spaces between them, then cook on high for 30 to 40 minutes or until the dumplings are light and fluffy. Spoon into shallow bowls to serve.

For sausage & ale stew with parsley dumplings, grill or broil 8 large sausages until browned but not cooked through, then add them to the slow-cooker pot with the vegetables and mixture of hot sauce and stock. Cook and serve as above.

thai beef curry

Preparation time **15 minutes**
Cooking temperature **low**
Cooking time **8 hours**
 5 minutes to 10 hours
 10 minutes
Serves **4**

14 fl oz can **full-fat**
 coconut milk
1 bunch of **scallions**,
 very finely chopped
3 tablespoons **laksa Thai**
 curry paste
3 **dried kaffir lime leaves**
2 tablespoons **jaggery (palm**
 sugar) or light brown sugar
2 tablespoons **rice vinegar**
2 teaspoons **fish sauce**
1 ½ lb **lean beef chuck**, cubed
1 ½ cups **snow peas**, trimmed

To serve
small handful of **cilantro**, torn
 into pieces
sliced **red chile**
lime wedges

Preheat the slow cooker if necessary; see the manufacturer's instructions. Pour the coconut milk into a saucepan, add the scallions, laksa paste, and lime leaves, then add the sugar, vinegar, and fish sauce. Bring to a boil, stirring.

Place the beef on the bottom of the slow-cooker pot, pour in the hot coconut broth, stir together, then press the beef beneath the surface of the liquid. Cover with the lid and cook on low for 8 to 10 hours until the beef is tender.

Stir the curry, scatter with the sliced snow peas, then re-cover and cook for 5 to 10 minutes until the snow peas are hot yet still crunchy. Ladle the curry into rice-lined bowls, if liked, and scatter with the cilantro and chile. Squeeze lime juice over to taste.

For Thai pumpkin & mushroom curry, omit the beef chuck and add 1 lb ready-prepared pumpkin or butternut squash cut into ¾-inch cubes and 3 cups halved mushrooms. Cook with the hot coconut broth on low for 7 to 8 hours until the vegetables are tender, then serve as above.

lamb ragù

Preparation time **15 minutes**
Cooking temperature **low**
Cooking time **8 to 9 hours**
Serves **4**

2½ cups ready-made **tomato
  and bell pepper ragù sauce**
½ cup **red wine** or **lamb stock**
10½ oz scrubbed **baby new
  potatoes**, thickly sliced
1¼ lb diced **lamb**
1 **red bell pepper**, cored,
  seeded, and cut into chunks
1 **yellow bell pepper**, cored,
  seeded, and cut into chunks

Preheat the slow cooker if necessary; see the manufacturer's instructions. Pour the ragù sauce and wine or stock into a saucepan and bring to a boil. Alternatively, heat the mixture in a microwave.

Place the potato slices on the bottom of the slow-cooker pot, arrange the lamb on top, then add the red and yellow bell peppers. Pour in the hot sauce, then cover with the lid and cook on low for 8 to 9 hours until the potatoes and lamb are tender.

Stir the ragù. Serve garnished with basil leaves and accompanied by warm garlic bread, if liked.

For beef & mushroom ragù, make the recipe as above adding 1¼ lb diced beef chuck instead of the lamb and 2 cups sliced mushrooms in place of the yellow bell pepper.

food to impress

baked red onions & herb couscous

Preparation time **25 minutes**
Cooking temperature **high**
Cooking time **4 to 5 hours**
Serves **4**

4 large **red onions**, peeled
½ lb **ground beef**
1 teaspoon **ground cinnamon**, divided
1 teaspoon **ground cumin**, divided
1 teaspoon **turmeric**, divided
2 tablespoons **currants**
14 oz can **diced tomatoes**
½ cup **vegetable stock**
2 **garlic cloves**, minced
2 teaspoons **light brown sugar**
salt and **pepper**

Herb couscous
1 cup **couscous**
1¾ cups **boiling water**
2 tablespoons **olive oil**
handful of **parsley**, chopped
handful of **cilantro**, chopped

Preheat the slow cooker if necessary; see the manufacturer's instructions. Cut a thin slice off the top of each onion and reserve. Hollow out the center of 1 onion to make a cup, then repeat with the other onions. (Reserve the scooped-out centers to use in other recipes.)

Put the ground beef in a bowl and stir in half the ground spices, then add the currants and a little salt and pepper and stir to combine. Spoon into the hollowed-out onions, then set the reserved onion lids back on top.

Heat the tomatoes, stock, garlic, and sugar with the remaining spices. Pour into the bottom of the slow-cooker pot, then add the onions. Cover with the lid and cook on high for 4 to 5 hours until the onions are tender.

Soak the couscous in the boiling water for 5 minutes. Add the oil, herbs, and a little salt and pepper and fluff up with a fork. Spoon onto plates, top with the onions, and serve with the sauce alongside.

For baked red bell peppers with herb couscous, halve 2 red bell peppers and scoop out the cores and seeds. Fill with the ground beef mixture, then arrange on top of the tomato mixture. Cook and serve as above.

vegetable biryani

Preparation time **25 minutes**
Cooking temperature **low**
Cooking time **4½ to 5½ hours**
Serves **4**

2 tablespoons **butter**
1 tablespoon **sunflower oil**
1 **onion**, chopped
1 **eggplant**, diced
2 tablespoons **mild curry paste**
1-inch piece of **fresh ginger root**, peeled and finely chopped
2 **garlic cloves**, minced
4 oz **green snap beans**, trimmed and cut into 3
1 cup **frozen peas**
1 cup **cherry tomatoes**, halved
1 cup **easy-cook long-grain white rice**, divided
3 **cardamom pods**, crushed
1 quart **boiling vegetable stock**
salt and **pepper**
handful of **cilantro**, torn into pieces, to garnish

To serve
2 tablespoons **butter**
¼ cup **sliced almonds**
¼ cup **cashews**

Preheat the slow cooker if necessary; see the manufacturer's instructions. Heat the butter and oil in a large skillet, add the onion and eggplant, and fry for 5 minutes, stirring, until both are lightly browned.

Mix in the curry paste, ginger, and garlic, then add the beans, peas, and tomatoes and season to taste.

Sprinkle half the rice over the bottom of the slow-cooker pot, spoon over the vegetable mix, then cover with the remaining rice, tucking the cardamom pods and their black seeds into the rice. Pour in the boiling stock, then cover with the lid and cook on low for 4½ to 5½ hours until the rice is tender.

Heat the butter in a skillet, add the nuts, and fry for 2 to 3 minutes, stirring, until golden. Spoon the biryani onto plates, scatter the nuts on top, and serve garnished with cilantro.

For salmon biryani, omit the eggplant and add the remaining vegetables to the fried onion. Sprinkle half the rice into the slow-cooker pot and arrange 4 pieces of salmon, weighing about 4 oz each, on top. Spoon over the onion mix, then the remaining rice. Add the stock, then cook and serve as above.

eggplant timbale

Preparation time **25 minutes**
Cooking temperature **high**
Cooking time **1½ to 2 hours**
Serves **2**

¼ cup **olive oil**, plus extra
  for greasing
1 large **eggplant**, thinly sliced
1 small **onion**, chopped
1 **garlic clove**, minced
½ teaspoon **ground
  cinnamon**
¼ teaspoon **grated nutmeg**
2½ tablespoons **pistachio
  nuts**, coarsely chopped
2½ tablespoons **pitted dates**,
  coarsely chopped
2½ tablespoons **ready-to-eat
  dried apricots**, coarsely
  chopped
½ cup **easy-cook long-
  grain rice**
1¼ cups **boiling vegetable
  stock**
salt and **pepper**

Preheat the slow cooker if necessary; see the manufacturer's instructions. Check that 2 soufflé dishes, each 12 fl oz, will fit in the slow-cooker pot. Oil the insides and line them with nonstick parchment paper.

Heat 1 tablespoon of the oil in a large skillet, add one-third of the eggplants, and fry on both sides until softened and golden. Transfer the eggplant slices to a plate. Repeat with the remaining eggplants slices using 2 more tablespoonfuls of the oil.

Heat the remaining oil in the pan, add the onion, and fry for 5 minutes or until soft. Stir in the garlic, spices, nuts, fruit, and rice. Season and and mix well.

Arrange one-third of the eggplant slices in the bottoms of the 2 dishes, overlapping the slices. Spoon one-quarter of the rice mixture into each dish, add a second layer of eggplant slices, then divide the remaining rice equally between the dishes. Top with the remaining eggplant slices. Pour the stock into the dishes, cover with lightly oiled foil, and put in the slow-cooker pot.

Pour boiling water into the pot to come halfway up the sides of the dishes. Cover with the lid and cook on high for 1½ to 2 hours or until the rice is tender. Lift the dishes out of the slow-cooker pot using oven mitts and remove the foil. Loosen the edges of the timbales with a knife, invert onto plates, and peel off the lining paper. Serve hot with arugula and baked tomatoes, if liked.

For curried eggplant timbale, omit the cinnamon and nutmeg and replace with 1 tablespoon mild curry paste. Continue as above. Serve with a side dish of creamy spinach.

tomato, pepper & garlic bruschetta

Preparation time **20 minutes**
Cooking temperature **high**
Cooking time **3 to 5 hours**
Serves **4**

1 large **red bell pepper**,
   quartered, cored, and
   seeded
1 lb **plum tomatoes**, halved
4 large **garlic cloves**,
   unpeeled
leaves from 2 to 3 **thyme
   sprigs**
1 teaspoon **superfine sugar**
1 tablespoon **extra virgin
   olive oil**

To serve
8 slices of **French stick**,
   about 6 oz in total
8 **pitted black olives in
   brine**, drained
salt and **pepper**

Preheat the slow cooker if necessary; see the manufacturer's instructions. Arrange the bell pepper pieces, skin-side down, in the bottom of the slow-cooker pot, arrange the tomatoes on top, then tuck the garlic in among them. Scatter the thyme leaves on top, reserving a little to garnish. Sprinkle with the sugar and drizzle with the oil.

Season to taste, cover with the lid, and cook on high for 3 to 5 hours until the vegetables are tender but the tomatoes still hold their shape.

Lift the vegetables out of the slow-cooker pot with a slotted spoon. Peel the skins off the bell peppers, tomatoes, and garlic, then coarsely chop the vegetables and toss together. Adjust the seasoning if necessary.

Toast the bread on both sides, then arrange on a serving plate. Spoon the tomato mixture on top. Arrange the olives and reserved thyme on the bruschetta and serve as a light lunch or appetizer.

For quick tomato & bell pepper pizzas, follow the recipe above to cook the tomato and bell pepper mixture, then spoon it onto 2 halved and toasted ciabatta rolls. Scatter with ½ cup shredded Cheddar cheese and place under a preheated hot broiler until the cheese is melted. Serve with salad.

seafood laksa

Preparation time **20 minutes**
Cooking temperature **low**
Cooking time **2¼ to 2½ hours**
Serves **4**

1 bunch of **scallions**

2 **hot green chiles**

1-inch piece of **fresh ginger root**, peeled and sliced

2 **garlic cloves**, sliced

2 handfuls of **cilantro**, coarsely torn, divided

2 tablespoons **sunflower oil**

14 fl oz can **full-fat coconut milk**

1 cup **fish stock**

2 teaspoons **jaggery (palm sugar)**

2 teaspoons **tamarind paste**

2 teaspoons **fish sauce**

½ teaspoon **turmeric**

2 **dried kaffir lime leaves**

10½ oz **cod fillet**

10½ oz **salmon fillet**

6 oz **cooked peeled shrimp**, rinsed and drained

10½ oz **bean sprouts**, rinsed and drained

12 oz package chilled **ready-cooked fine rice noodles**

¼ **cucumber**, cut into thin shreds

Preheat the slow cooker if necessary; see the manufacturer's instructions. Trim and quarter the scallions. Halve the chiles lengthwise and seed them. Finely chop the onions, chile, garlic, and half the cilantro in a food processor, if using, or with a large knife.

Heat half of the oil in a skillet, add the chopped onion mixture, and fry over low heat for 3 to 4 minutes until just softened. Stir in the coconut milk, stock, sugar, tamarind paste, and fish sauce, then mix in the turmeric and kaffir lime leaves. Bring to a boil, stirring.

Halve and skin the fish fillets and arrange them snugly together in the bottom of the slow-cooker pot in a single layer. Pour in the hot coconut broth, then cover with the lid and cook on low for 2 to 2¼ hours until the fish is cooked through.

Break the fish into large pieces and add the shrimp. Cover and cook for 15 minutes until the shrimp are piping hot. Meanwhile, heat the remaining oil in a wok or large skillet, add the bean sprouts and noodles, and stir-fry for 2 to 3 minutes. Spoon the mixture into large shallow serving bowls.

Ladle the fish and broth into the bowls, then garnish with the remaining cilantro and the shreds of cucumber. Serve immediately.

For beef laksa, add vegetable stock in place of the fish stock and 1¼ lb trimmed and thinly sliced rump steak instead of the cod, salmon, and shrimp. Cook and serve as above.

three-fish gratin

Preparation time **20 minutes**
Cooking temperature **low**
Cooking time **2 to 3 hours**
Serves **4**

2 tablespoons **cornstarch**
1¾ cups **whole milk**, divided
½ cup shredded **sharp Cheddar cheese**
3 tablespoons chopped **parsley**
1 **leek**, thinly sliced
1 **bay leaf**
1 lb **mixed skinless fish**, such as salmon, cod, and smoked haddock, diced
salt and **pepper**

Topping
½ cup **fresh bread crumbs**
½ cup shredded **sharp Cheddar cheese**

Preheat the slow cooker if necessary; see the manufacturer's instructions. Place the cornstarch in a saucepan with a little of the milk and mix to a smooth paste. Stir in the remaining milk, then add the cheese, parsley, leek, and bay leaf. Season to taste and bring to a boil, stirring. Cook until thickened.

Place the fish in the slow-cooker pot. Pour the hot leek sauce evenly over the fish, cover, and cook on low for 2 to 3 hours until the fish is cooked through.

Transfer the fish mixture to a shallow baking dish, sprinkle the bread crumbs and shredded cheese evenly over the top, then place under a preheated hot broiler for 4 to 5 minutes until golden brown. Serve with steamed snow peas, if liked.

For fish pies, follow the recipe above, omitting the bread crumb and cheese topping. Peel and cut 1¼ lb potatoes into chunks. Cook the potatoes in a saucepan of lightly salted boiling water for 15 minutes or until tender. Drain and mash with ¼ cup skim milk, then season and stir in ½ cup shredded sharp Cheddar cheese. Divide the cooked fish mixture among 4 single-serving pie dishes, spoon the mashed potatoes on top, rough up the surface with a fork, then brush with 1 beaten egg. Place under a preheated medium broiler and cook until golden.

chicken ramen

Preparation time **20 minutes**
Cooking temperature **low**
and **high**
Cooking time **6¼ to 8½ hours**
Serves **4**

1¼ quarts **boiling chicken stock**
3 tablespoons **soy sauce**, plus extra to serve
2 teaspoons **fish sauce**
2 teaspoons **superfine sugar**
½ to 1 teaspoon **crushed red chile flakes** (to taste)
2 to 3 **garlic cloves**, minced
2-inch piece of **fresh ginger root**, thinly sliced
4 **scallions**, sliced
2 **star anise**
2 **dried kaffir lime leaves** (optional)
1¼ lb **skinless, boneless chicken thighs**, diced
4 oz **instant plain** or **chicken ramen noodles** (discard the flavoring sachet if using chicken noodles)
10½ oz **edamame bean stir-fry mix**
handful of **cilantro leaves**

Preheat the slow cooker if necessary; see the manufacturer's instructions. Mix the boiling chicken stock with the soy sauce, fish sauce, and sugar, then mix in the chile flakes to taste, the garlic, ginger, scallions, star anise, and kaffir lime leaves, if using.

Put the diced chicken into the slow-cooker pot and pour in the boiling stock mixture. Cover with the lid and cook on low for 6 to 8 hours until the chicken is cooked through.

Increase the heat to high, then stir in the noodles and stir-fry vegetables. Cook for 15 to 30 minutes until the noodles are hot and the vegetables are just beginning to soften.

Stir in the cilantro, then ladle into deep bowls and serve with extra soy sauce.

For salmon ramen, omit the chicken stock and chicken and replace with fish or 1¼ quarts boiling vegetable stock and 4 pieces of salmon, each weighing 4 oz. Cook on low for 1½ to 2 hours until the salmon is cooked through. Lift the salmon out, break it into flakes, and return it to the pot with the noodles and edamame bean stir-fry mix. Continue as above.

red thai chicken curry

Preparation time **20 minutes**
Cooking temperature **low**
Cooking time **8¼ to 9½ hours**
Serves **4**

1 tablespoon **sunflower oil**
1 **onion**, finely chopped
2 tablespoons **red Thai**
   curry paste
2 teaspoons **galangal paste**
14 fl oz can **full-fat coconut**
   milk
1 cup **chicken stock**
2 teaspoons **fish sauce**
2 teaspoons **light brown**
   sugar
2 **dried kaffir lime leaves**
1¼ lb **skinless, boneless**
   chicken thighs, cut into
   chunks
4 oz **baby corn cobs**,
   thickly sliced
10½ oz **asparagus**, each
   spear trimmed and cut into
   3 slices
3 oz **snow peas**, halved
1 **carrot**, cut into matchsticks
cilantro leaves, coarsely
   chopped, to garnish

Preheat the slow cooker if necessary; see the
manufacturer's instructions. Heat the sunflower oil in
a saucepan, add the onion, and fry it over medium heat
for 2 to 3 minutes. Stir in the curry paste and galangal,
then mix in the coconut milk, stock, fish sauce, sugar,
and lime leaves and bring to a boil, stirring.

Add the chicken to the slow-cooker pot, pour in the
coconut milk mixture, and make sure the chicken is
below the liquid. Cover with the lid and cook on low for
8 to 9 hours until the chicken is cooked through.

Stir the curry, then add the vegetables and cook for
15 to 30 minutes until the vegetables are hot but still
have a little bite.

Ladle into rice-lined bowls, if liked, and garnish with
coarsely chopped cilantro leaves.

For red Thai beef curry, omit the chicken and add
1¼ lb trimmed and cubed beef chuck. Cook and serve
as above.

duck confit

Preparation time **40 minutes,**
  plus salting **4 hours** or
  overnight
Cooking temperature **high**
Cooking time **3½ to 4 hours**
Serves **4**

4 **duck legs**, about 7 oz each
3 tablespoons **coarse sea salt**
10½ oz jar **duck fat**, plus extra
  if needed
4 **garlic cloves**, sliced
2 **rosemary sprigs**
2 **thyme sprigs**
coarsely crushed **black pepper**

Place the duck in a single layer in a shallow dish and sprinkle with the salt. Chill for 4 hours or overnight.

Brush the salt from the duck and discard any juices in the dish. Preheat the slow cooker if necessary; see the manufacturer's instructions. Spoon the duck fat into the bottom of the slow-cooker pot, add the garlic, herbs, and black pepper, then press the duck pieces down into the fat so that they fit together snugly in a single layer.

Cover with the lid and cook on high for 3½ to 4 hours or until the duck is cooked and falling off the bone.

Lift the duck out of the slow cooker and pack it into a large, wide-mouth jar, pressing it down to minimize any air pockets. Strain the fat into the jar so that the top duck piece is well covered and any air pockets between the pieces of meat are filled with fat. If there isn't quite enough, top off with a little extra melted duck fat.

Cover with a lid and let cool, then transfer to the refrigerator and store for up to 1 week. When ready to serve, remove the duck pieces from the fat, scraping off most of the fat. Roast in a preheated oven, 425°F, for 20 minutes until crisp and piping hot. Serve with a watercress, Belgian endive, and orange salad, if liked, and potatoes roasted in duck fat (see below).

For potatoes roasted in duck fat, to serve as a side, cut 1 ½ lb peeled potatoes into ¾-inch chunks, parboil for 4 to 5 minutes, then drain well. Melt ¼ cup of the duck fat in a roasting pan for 4 to 5 minutes, add the potatoes, and toss to coat in the fat. Roast in a preheated oven, 425°F, for 30 to 35 minutes, turning once, until golden.

madeira-braised pheasant

Preparation time **25 minutes**
Cooking temperature **low**
Cooking time **7 to 8 hours**
Serves **4**

2 **hen pheasants** or 1 **hen**
   and 1 **small cock pheasant**
   (ensure they will fit in the
   slow-cooker pot)
2 tablespoons **butter**
1 tablespoon **olive oil**
2 **onions**, cut into wedges
4 oz **smoked bacon**, diced
½ cup **Madeira** or **extra
   chicken stock**, if preferred
1¼ cups **chicken stock**
1 tablespoon **redcurrant jelly**
2½ cups sliced **mushrooms**
3 **thyme sprigs**
salt and **pepper**

Preheat the slow cooker if necessary; see the manufacturer's instructions. Season inside the body cavity of each pheasant with salt and pepper.

Heat the butter and oil in a large skillet, add the pheasants, breast-side down, and fry over medium heat until they are golden. Lift them out of the pan and put them on a plate.

Add the onion wedges and bacon to the pan and fry for 4 to 5 minutes, stirring, until golden. Pour in the Madeira, if using, stock, and redcurrant jelly and bring to a boil, stirring, until the jelly has dissolved. Season with salt and pepper.

Add the pheasants to the slow-cooker pot, breast-side down. If they are very snug, you may need to put them into the pot sideways. Add the mushrooms and thyme sprigs, then pour in the hot onion mixture.

Cover with the lid and cook on low for 7 to 8 hours or until the meat is beginning to come away from the bones and the juices run clear when the birds are pierced through the thickest part with a skewer or small knife.

Lift the birds out of the slow-cooker pot and place them on a large plate. Scoop out the onions, bacon and mushrooms with a slotted spoon, place in a bowl, cover with foil, and keep hot. Strain the stock mixture into a large skillet and boil for 5 to 10 minutes until reduced and thickened.

Carve the breast meat and arrange it in shallow bowls. Spoon the onion, bacon, and mushroom mixture over it, and serve with the sauce and mashed potatoes and green cabbage, if liked.

jerk pork with pineapple salsa

Preparation time **20 minutes**
Cooking temperature **high**
Cooking time **5 to 6 hours**
Serves **4**

1½ to 1¾ lb **bone-in pork
    shoulder roast**
2 tablespoons **powdered
    jerk spice mix**
4 teaspoons **light brown
    sugar**
1 **onion**, coarsely chopped
1 **carrot**, sliced
1 cup **boiling chicken stock**
salt and **pepper**

Pineapple salsa
1 small **pineapple**, trimmed
    and peeled
2 teaspoons **light brown
    sugar**
1 large **red chile**, halved,
    seeded, and minced
grated zest of 1 **lime**

Preheat the slow cooker if necessary; see the
manufacturer's directions. Remove the string from
the pork, then cut off the skin. Unroll and, if needed,
make a slit in the meat so that it can be opened out
to make a strip that is of an even thickness.

Rub the pork all over with the jerk spice mix, sugar,
and salt and pepper. Put the pork in the slow-cooker
pot, then scatter the onion and carrot into the gaps
around the pork. Pour the boiling stock around the pork.
Cover with the lid and cook on high for 5 to 6 hours
until the meat is very tender and almost falls apart.

Meanwhile, slice the pineapple, cut out and discard
the core, then finely chop the flesh. Put it into a bowl
with the sugar, chile, and lime zest. Mix together, then
cover and chill until the pork is ready.

Lift the pork out of the slow-cooker pot, remove any fat,
then shred the meat with 2 forks. Serve with the salsa
and rice mixed with canned black-eye peas, if liked.

For harissa pork with minted couscous, spread
the pork with 4 teaspoons harissa, sugar, and salt and
pepper, add onion, carrot, and stock and cook as above.
Serve with 1 cup couscous soaked in 1¾ cups boiling
water for 5 minutes, then mix with the grated zest and
juice of 1 lemon, 2 tablespoons olive oil, and a handful
of chopped mint and 3 finely chopped scallions.

lettuce wrappers

Preparation time **20 minutes**
Cooking temperature **low**
Cooking time **8 to 9 hours**
Serves **4**

1 tablespoon **sunflower oil**
1½ lb **beef chuck**, cut into
small cubes
1 **onion**, chopped
2 **garlic cloves**, minced
2 tablespoons **all-purpose
flour**
1½ cups **beef stock**
1 teaspoon **crushed red
chile flakes**
½ teaspoon **chili powder**
2 tablespoons **soy sauce**
2 tablespoons **hoisin sauce**
2 tablespoons **rice vinegar**
1 tablespoon **dark brown
sugar**
salt and **pepper**

To serve
1 **iceberg lettuce**
1 small **red onion**, thinly sliced
small handful of **cilantro**,
coarsely chopped

Preheat the slow cooker if necessary; see the manufacturer's instructions. Heat the oil in a large skillet, add the beef a few pieces at a time, then fry over high heat, stirring, until browned.

Add the onion and garlic and fry for 3 to 4 minutes until softened. Sprinkle with the flour and mix it in, then gradually stir in the stock. Scatter with the crushed chile flakes and chili powder, then stir in the soy and hoisin sauces, vinegar, and sugar. Season with a little pepper.

Bring to a boil, then transfer to the slow-cooker pot. Press the meat beneath the liquid, cover with the lid, and cook on low for 8 to 9 hours until the beef is tender.

Separate the lettuce leaves, spoon a little of the beef into each lettuce cup, then scatter with the red onion slices and chopped cilantro. To eat, fold the leaves over the beef filling and pick up the parcels with your fingers or eat them with a knife and fork.

For beef "Peking duck" wrappers, make and cook the beef as above. Warm 16 Chinese pancakes in a steamer according to the package instructions. Separate the pancakes, top with spoonfuls of the hot beef, ½ cucumber cut into matchstick strips, and 1 bunch of scallions, cut into matchstick strips. Roll up and serve immediately.

sunday best beef

Preparation time **20 minutes**
Cooking temperature **low**
Cooking time **8 to 9 hours**
Serves **4**

2 tablespoons **all-purpose
 flour**
1½ lb piece of **blade steak**,
 cut into ¾-inch thick slices
2 tablespoons **olive oil**
10½ oz **shallots**, peeled
½ cup **red wine** or **extra beef
 stock**, if preferred
1¼ cups **beef stock**
1 tablespoon **tomato paste**
1 teaspoon **dried mixed
 herbs**
1 teaspoon **Dijon mustard**
2 cups sliced **mushrooms**
salt and **pepper**

To serve
4 large ready-made
 Yorkshire puddings
new potatoes
selection of vegetables

Preheat the slow cooker if necessary; see the manufacturer's instructions. Mix the flour and a little salt and pepper together on a plate, then coat both sides of the beef slices with the seasoned flour.

Heat 1 tablespoon of the oil in a large skillet, add the beef slices, and fry until browned on both sides. Lift out the beef and transfer it to the slow-cooker pot. Add the remaining oil and fry the shallots for a few minutes until they are just beginning to brown.

Sprinkle with any remaining seasoned flour, then mix in the wine, if using, stock, tomato paste, herbs, and mustard. Bring to a boil, stirring constantly.

Add the mushrooms to the slow-cooker pot, then pour in the shallot mixture. Press the beef below the surface of the liquid, cover with the lid, and cook on low for 8 to 9 hours or until the beef is tender.

When almost ready to serve, heat the Yorkshire puddings in the oven according to the package instructions. Steam the vegetables, then transfer the Yorkshire puddings to serving plates and fill them with the beef, sauce, and steamed vegetables.

For poor man's Sunday best, grill or broil 8 large pork sausages until browned but not cooked through. Add to the slow-cooker pot. Fry the shallots in a little oil, sprinkle with the flour, then add ½ cup canned tomato puree instead of the wine, stir in the remaining ingredients, and cook and serve as above.

lamb & mushroom pudding

Preparation time **35 minutes**
Cooking temperature **high**
Cooking time **5 to 6 hours**
Serves **4**

2 tablespoons **butter**, plus
extra for greasing
1 tablespoon **olive oil**
1 **onion**, thinly sliced
2 cups sliced **mushrooms**
1 lb diced **lamb**
1 tablespoon **Worcestershire
sauce**
5 tablespoons **ruby port** or
red wine or **extra lamb
stock**, if preferred
5 tablespoons **lamb stock**
leaves from **2 rosemary
sprigs**, chopped
salt and **pepper**

Pastry
2½ cups **all-purpose flour**
sifted with 2½ teaspoons
baking powder
¾ cup **vegetable shortening**
leaves from 3 **rosemary
sprigs**, chopped
1 cup **cold water**

Preheat the slow cooker if necessary; see the manufacturer's instructions. Grease a 1¼ quart steamed pudding mold. Heat the butter and oil in a skillet, add the onion, and fry for 5 minutes until golden. Add the mushrooms and lamb and fry for 5 minutes, stirring, until browned. Add the Worcestershire sauce, port or wine, if using, stock, and rosemary. Season and set aside.

Make the pastry. Place the flour, shortening, and rosemary in a large bowl, season generously, and stir together. Gradually mix in the cold water to make a soft but not sticky dough, adding extra if needed. Lightly knead the dough, then roll it out thickly on a lightly floured surface to make a rough circle about 13 inches in diameter. Cut a one-quarter wedge out of the circle and reserve this for the lid. Lift the remaining piece into the pudding mold, butting the cut edges together, then press together to seal and press the pastry over the mold.

Spoon the lamb mixture into the mold. Pat and roll the reserved pastry into a circle the same size as the top of the mold, stick it in place with a little water, then trim off any excess. Cover with a dome of buttered foil, then stand the mold in the slow-cooker pot. Pour boiling water into the slow-cooker pot so it reaches halfway up the sides of the mold. Cover and cook on high for 5 to 6 hours until the pastry is light and fluffy and the lamb is tender. Lift the mold out of the slow cooker with oven mitts. Serve with mashed turnips and carrots, if liked.

For steak & mushroom pudding, replace the lamb with 1 lb sliced rump steak and add ½ cup beer or extra stock and 2 teaspoons light brown sugar in place of the port and thyme. Make as above.

rioja-braised lamb with olives

Preparation time **20 minutes**
Cooking temperature **high**
Cooking time **5 to 6 hours**
Serves **4**

2 tablespoons **olive oil**,
   divided
4 **lamb shanks**, weighing
   3 lb in total
2 **red onions**, cut into wedges
4 large **garlic cloves**, halved
1 ¼ cups **Rioja red wine** or
   lamb stock
14 oz can **diced tomatoes**
1 tablespoon **redcurrant jelly**
3 **rosemary sprigs**
1 ¼ cups **mixed pitted olives**
salt and **pepper**

Preheat the slow cooker if necessary; see the manufacturer's instructions. Heat 1 tablespoon of the oil in a large skillet, season the lamb shanks, then add them to the pan and brown on all sides. Lift them out of the pan and put them in the slow-cooker pot with the meatiest parts downward.

Add the remaining oil and onion wedges to the pan and fry for 3 to 4 minutes until just beginning to color. Add the garlic, wine or stock, tomatoes, redcurrant jelly, and rosemary. Season with salt and pepper and bring to a boil, stirring.

Scatter the olives over the lamb, then pour in the hot onion mixture. Cover with the lid and cook on high for 5 to 6 hours until the lamb is very tender.

When ready to serve, pour the liquid out of the slow cooker into a saucepan and boil for 10 minutes until reduced by half. Put the lamb into shallow bowls lined with some runny polenta flavored with butter and Parmesan, or mashed potatoes, if liked, spoon over the onions and olives, then serve with the Rioja sauce.

For Rioja-braised chicken with olives, substitute a chicken, weighing about 3 lb, for the lamb shanks and cook as above, with the chicken placed breast-side down in the liquid, until the chicken is cooked through.

peppered venison cobbler

Preparation time **35 minutes**
Cooking temperature **low**
and **high**
Cooking time **8¾ to 11 hours**
Serves **4**

2 tablespoons **butter**
1 tablespoon **olive oil**
1½ lb diced **venison**
1 large **red onion**, sliced
2 cups sliced **mushrooms**
2 **garlic cloves**, chopped
2 tablespoons **all-purpose
flour**
1 cup **red wine** or **extra
chicken stock**
1 cup **chicken stock**
2 teaspoons **tomato paste**
2 tablespoons **redcurrant jelly**
1 teaspoon crushed **peppercorns**
salt

Cobbler
2 cups **all-purpose flour**
2 teaspoons **baking powder**
3 tablespoons **butter**, diced
4 oz **Gorgonzola cheese**,
finely crumbled
3 tablespoons chopped
parsley or **chives**
1 **egg**, beaten
4 to 5 tablespoons **milk**

Preheat the slow cooker if necessary; see the manufacturer's instructions. Heat the butter and oil in a large skillet, add the diced venison a few pieces at time, then fry until evenly browned. Transfer to a plate.

Add the onion to the pan and fry for 5 minutes. Stir in the mushrooms, garlic, and flour and cook for 1 minute. Stir in the wine, if using, stock, tomato paste, redcurrant jelly, peppercorns, and salt and bring to a boil.

Arrange the venison in the slow-cooker pot, add the hot stock mixture, and press the venison below the surface. Cover with the lid and cook on low for 8 to 10 hours until the venison is tender.

When the venison is tender, make the cobbler topping. Sift the flour with the baking powder in a bowl. Add the butter and rub it into the flour mixture with your fingertips until it resembles fine bread crumbs. Stir in a little salt and pepper, the cheese, and herbs. Reserve 1 tablespoon of egg for glazing and add the rest. Gradually mix in enough milk to make a soft dough.

Knead lightly, then pat the dough into a thick oval or a disk that is a little smaller than the top of your slow cooker. Cut it into 8 wedges and arrange these, spaced slightly apart, on top of the venison. Cover and cook on high for 45 minutes to 1 hour until the dough topping has turned golden.

Lift the pot out of the machine using oven mitts, and brush the cobbler with the reserved egg. Brown the top under a preheated hot broiler. Serve with green snap beans, if liked.

nostalgic desserts

apple & pecan cake

Preparation time **30 minutes**,
plus cooling
Cooking temperature **high**
Cooking time **3½ to 4 hours**
Serves **6**

1 stick **butter**, plus extra
for greasing
½ cup packed **light brown
sugar**
¼ cup **light corn syrup**
1¼ cups **all-purpose flour**
1¼ teaspoons **baking powder**
1 teaspoon **baking soda**
1 teaspoon **ground cinnamon**
1 teaspoon **ground ginger**
2 **eggs**, beaten
1 **apple**, cored and grated
(no need to peel)
½ cup **pecans**, broken into
pieces, plus extra to serve
9 oz **cream cheese**
½ cup **powdered sugar**,
sifted, plus extra to decorate
½ teaspoon **orange extract**

Preheat the slow cooker if necessary; see the manufacturer's instructions. Butter a soufflé dish with a diameter of 6 inches and 3¼ inches high. Line the bottom with nonstick parchment paper.

Heat the butter, sugar, and syrup together in a saucepan over very low heat. Remove the pan from the heat to cool slightly.

Sift the flour, baking powder, baking soda, and ground spices together, then stir into the butter mixture with the beaten eggs and grated apple. Mix until smooth, then stir in the pecans.

Pour the batter into the buttered dish, cover with a dome of buttered foil, and stand in the slow-cooker pot. Pour boiling water into the cooker pot around the dish so that it reaches halfway up the sides of the dish. Cover with the lid and cook on high for 3½ to 4 hours or until well risen and a skewer comes out clean when inserted into the cake.

Lift out the soufflé dish with oven mitts, remove the foil, and let cool for 15 minutes. Loosen the edge of the cake, invert onto a wire rack, and peel off the lining paper. Let cool completely.

When ready to serve, beat the cream cheese, powdered sugar, and orange extract together. Transfer the cake to a serving plate, spread the frosting evenly over the top and sides of the cake, and scatter with the extra broken pecans. Dust with sifted powdered sugar.

For carrot & walnut cake, omit the apple and pecan nuts and add 1¼ cups grated carrot and ½ cup chopped walnuts. Cook as above.

strawberry cheesecake

Preparation time **30 minutes**,
 plus chilling
Cooking temperature **high**
Cooking time **2 to 2½ hours**
Serves **4 to 5**

4 **plain, round vanilla,
 sponge,** or **pound cakes,**
 5½ inches in diameter, or
 1 slab of cake cut to size
10½ oz **regular cream
 cheese**
¼ cup **superfine sugar**
½ cup **heavy cream**
3 **eggs**
grated zest and juice of
 ½ **lemon**

Topping
2 tablespoons **strawberry jam**
1 tablespoon **lemon juice**
1¼ cups **strawberries,** hulled
 and sliced

Preheat the slow cooker if necessary; see the manufacturer's instructions. Line the bottom and sides of a soufflé dish, 5½ inches in diameter and 3½ inches high, with nonstick parchment paper, checking first that it will fit in the slow-cooker pot. Line the bottom with the cake, trimming to fit in a single layer.

Put the cream cheese and sugar in a bowl, then gradually beat in the cream until smooth and thick. Gradually beat in the eggs 1 at a time, then mix in the lemon zest and juice. Pour the mixture into the dish and level the surface with a metal spatula.

Cover the top with buttered foil and lower it into the slow-cooker pot. Pour boiling water into the pot to come halfway up the sides of the dish. Cover with the lid and cook on high for 2 to 2½ hours or until the cheesecake is well risen and softly set in the center.

Lift the dish out of the slow-cooker pot using oven mitts and let the cheesecake stand to cool and become firm. It will sink quickly as it cools. Transfer to the refrigerator to chill for at least 4 hours.

Loosen the edge of the cheesecake with a knife, invert onto a serving plate, peel off the lining paper, and turn the cake the right way up. Mix the jam and lemon juice in a bowl until smooth, add the sliced strawberries, and toss together. Spoon the strawberry mixture on top of the cheesecake and serve immediately.

For blueberry cheesecake, mix 2 tablespoons blueberry jam with 1 tablespoon orange juice and 1 cup blueberries. Spoon the mixture over the cooled cheesecake and serve immediately.

christmas pudding

Preparation time **20 minutes**
Cooking temperature **high**
Cooking time **7 to 8 hours**
Reheating time **2 to 2½ hours**
Serves **6 to 8**

butter, for greasing
1 ½ lb **high-quality mixed
    dried fruit** (with larger
    fruits diced)
½ cup **pistachios**, chopped
2 tablespoons finely chopped
    candied or **stem ginger**
1 **apple**, peeled, cored, and
    coarsely grated
grated zest and juice of
    1 **lemon**
grated zest and juice of
    1 **orange**
¼ cup **brandy**, plus another
    ¼ cup to serve (optional)
¼ cup packed **soft dark
    brown sugar**
½ cup **all-purpose flour**
    sifted with ½ teaspoon
    baking powder
¾ cup **bread crumbs**
½ cup **vegetable shortening**
1 teaspoon **ground mixed
    spice**
2 **eggs**, beaten

Preheat the slow cooker if necessary; see the manufacturer's instructions. Check that a 1 ½ quart steamed pudding mold will fit inside your slow-cooker pot with a little room to spare, then butter the inside of the mold and then line the bottom with nonstick parchment paper.

Put the dried fruit, nuts, ginger, and grated apple into a large bowl. Add the citrus zests and juice and brandy and mix together well. Stir in the remaining ingredients. Spoon into the buttered mold, pressing down well. Cover with a large circle of nonstick parchment paper, then a piece of foil. Tie the foil to the mold with string and add a string handle. Lower the mold into the slow-cooker pot using foil straps (see page 15) and pour boiling water into the pot to come two-thirds of the way up the sides of the mold. Cover with the lid and cook on high for 7 to 8 hours. Check halfway through cooking and top off with extra boiling water if needed. Take out of the slow cooker and let cool.

Cover with fresh foil, leaving the parchment paper in place. Re-tie with string and keep in a cool place for 2 months or until Christmas.

When ready to serve, preheat the slow cooker, if needed, add the pudding and boiling water as above, and reheat on high for 2 to 2½ hours. Remove the foil and paper, loosen the pudding, and turn it out. Warm the brandy in a saucepan, if using. When it is just boiling, ignite with a long-handled match and quickly pour over the pudding. Serve with brandy butter or cream, if liked.

chocolate & guinness sponge cake

Preparation time **35 minutes**,
  plus cooling
Cooking temperature **high**
Cooking time **2 to 2½ hours**
Serves **6**

½ stick **butter**, softened,
  plus extra for greasing
1½ tablespoons unsweetened
  cocoa powder, plus extra
  for dusting
1½ cups **all-purpose flour**
1 teaspoon **baking soda**
½ teaspoon **baking powder**
¾ cup packed **brown sugar**
2 **eggs**
1 cup **Guinness**

Sauce
½ cup **Guinness**
¼ cup packed **brown sugar**
3½ oz **semisweet chocolate**,
  broken into pieces
1 teaspoon **cornstarch** mixed
  to a paste with a little water

Topping
2 tablespoons **light brown
  sugar**
1¼ cups **heavy cream**
3 oz **white chocolate**

Preheat the slow cooker if necessary; see the manufacturer's instructions. Grease a round baking dish with a diameter of 6 inches and 3¼ inches deep. Line the bottom with nonstick parchment paper.

Sift the cocoa powder, flour, baking soda, and baking powder together in a bowl. Cream the butter and sugar together in a separate large bowl or using a food processor. Beat in the eggs 1 at a time until smooth. Then add the cocoa mixture and gradually beat in the Guinness until smooth.

Spoon the batter into the prepared dish. Cover with a dome of buttered foil and place in the slow-cooker pot. Pour boiling water around the baking dish so that it reaches halfway up the sides of the dish. Cover and cook on high for 2 to 2½ hours until the cake is well risen and a skewer inserted into the center comes out clean.

Lift the baking dish out of the slow-cooker pot with oven mitts and let stand for 20 minutes. Loosen the cake edge and invert the cake onto a wire rack. Peel off the lining paper and let the cake cool completely.

Put all the sauce ingredients into a small saucepan and heat gently until the chocolate has melted, then bring just to a boil, stirring, until thickened. Remove the pan from the heat, cover, and let the sauce cool. For the topping, stir the sugar into the cream and chill in the refrigerator. Cut the cake in half horizontally, whisk the cream until it forms soft swirls, then spread on top of the cakes. Set the cakes separately on a cake board. Coarsely grate the white chocolate on top and dust with sifted cocoa. Cut into wedges and serve drizzled with the warmed sauce.

peach & raspberry cobbler

Preparation time **25 minutes**
Cooking temperature **high**
Cooking time **2½ to 3¼ hours**
Serves **6**

6 **peaches,** about 1½ lb in
   total, halved, stone removed,
   and flesh cut into chunks
¼ cup **superfine sugar**
juice of 1 **lemon**
2 cups **raspberries**

Topping
1 cup **all-purpose flour**
1 teaspoon **baking powder**
¼ cup **superfine sugar**
grated zest of 1 **lemon**
½ stick **butter,** cubed
1 **egg,** beaten, divided
¼ cup **skim milk**
sifted **powdered sugar,**
   for dusting

Preheat the slow cooker if necessary; see the manufacturer's instructions. Add the peach flesh, sugar, and lemon juice to the slow-cooker pot. Cover and cook on high for 1½ to 2 hours or until the peaches have softened.

Make the topping. Sift the flour and the baking powder together into a mixing bowl, then add the sugar, lemon zest, and butter. Rub the butter into the flour mixture with your fingertips or an electric stand mixer until the mixture resembles fine bread crumbs. Stir in half the egg (reserve the rest for glazing) and enough milk to blend to a soft, spoonable mixture.

Stir the peaches, then scatter them with the raspberries. Spoon the cobbler topping evenly in dollops on top of the fruit. Cover with the lid and cook on high for 1 to 1¼ hours until the topping is risen and set.

Take the pot out of the machine with oven mitts, brush the top with the remaining egg, then brown under a preheated hot broiler. Dust with a little sifted powdered sugar and serve hot with vanilla ice cream, if liked.

For apple & berry cobbler, put 1½ lb cooking apples, peeled, cored, and cut into chunks, in a slow-cooker pot with ½ cup sugar and lemon juice. Cook as above, then stir in 1 cup raspberries and 1 cup blackberries, then add the cobbler topping. Continue as above.

plum & blueberry betty

Preparation time **20 minutes**
Cooking temperature **high**
Cooking time **2½ to 3 hours**
Serves **6**

1 lb **red plums**, halved, pitted,
  and sliced
1 cup **blueberries**
½ cup **superfine sugar**
juice of 1 **orange**
3 tablespoons **water**

Topping
½ stick **butter**
3½ oz **white bread**, torn into
  small pieces
¼ cup **turbinado sugar**
½ cup **sliced almonds**
large pinch of **ground
  cinnamon**

Preheat the slow cooker if necessary; see the
manufacturer's instructions. Add the plums and
blueberries to the slow-cooker pot, sprinkle with the
sugar, then add the orange juice and measurement
water. Cover with the lid and cook on high for 2½ to
3 hours until the fruit is soft.

When almost ready to serve, heat the butter in a skillet,
add the bread, sugar, and almonds, sprinkle with a little
cinnamon, and fry over medium heat, stirring, until the
bread and almonds are crisp and golden.

Ladle the fruit into bowls, scatter with the topping, and
serve with scoops of vanilla ice cream, if liked.

For mixed berry Betty, add 2½ cups hulled and
halved strawberries to the slow-cooker pot with 1¼
cups raspberries and 1 cup blueberries, then add the
sugar and orange juice, omitting the water. Cook and
serve as above.

sticky toffee pudding

Preparation time **25 minutes**, plus standing
Cooking temperature **high**
Cooking time **2½ to 3 hours**
Serves **6**

¾ cup chopped **pitted dates**
1 teaspoon **baking soda**
2 cups **boiling water**
½ stick **butter**, at room temperature, plus extra for greasing
1½ cups **all-purpose flour**
1 teaspoon **baking powder**
½ cup packed **light brown sugar**
1 **egg**
1 teaspoon **vanilla extract**

Toffee sauce
½ stick **butter**
½ cup packed **light brown sugar**
½ cup **heavy cream**

Put the dates and baking soda in a small bowl. Stir in the boiling water, then let stand for 30 minutes. Grease a soufflé dish or ramekin with a diameter of 6 inches or a 5-cup round baking dish with a little butter.

Preheat the slow cooker if necessary; see the manufacturer's instructions. Sift the flour and baking powder together in a bowl. Cream the butter and sugar in a large bowl or food processor, then beat in the egg and vanilla until smooth. Add the flour and soaked dates, along with any soaking liquid, and beat well.

Spoon the mixture into the buttered dish, level off the surface, then cover with a domed piece of buttered foil. Place the dish in the slow-cooker pot, then pour boiling water around the dish so that it reaches halfway up the sides. Cover with the lid and cook on high for 2½ to 3 hours or until the pudding is deep brown, well risen, the top is dry, and a skewer inserted into the center comes out clean. Take the pudding out of the slow cooker with oven mitts.

Put all the sauce ingredients in a saucepan and heat gently, stirring, until the sugar has dissolved and the butter has melted. Increase the heat slightly and cook for 2 to 3 minutes, stirring constantly, until the sauce has thickened slightly and smells like toffee. Let it cool a little, then spoon the pudding into bowls, drizzle with the hot sauce, and serve with vanilla ice cream, if liked.

For sticky chocolate toffee pudding, sift 1 cup all-purpose flour together with 1 tablespoon unsweetened cocoa powder. Mix this with the baking powder, then make as above.

pineapple & rum upside-down cake

Preparation time **20 minutes**
Cooking temperature **high**
Cooking time **4 to 4½ hours**
Serves **6**

butter, for greasing
3 tablespoons **light brown sugar**
2 x 7½ oz cans **pineapple slices**, drained
about 6 **candied cherries**
3 tablespoons **light corn syrup**
2 tablespoons **dark rum**

Sponge cake
½ cup **soft margarine**
½ cup packed **light brown sugar**
1½ cups **all-purpose flour** sifted with 1½ teaspoons **baking powder**
2 teaspoons **ground ginger**
2 **eggs**
1 tablespoon **dark rum**

Preheat the slow cooker if necessary; see the manufacturer's instructions. Lightly butter a 1.5 quart steamed pudding mold. Line the bottom with nonstick parchment paper and grease the parchment paper, too. Sprinkle the sugar into the bottom and up the sides.

Line the inside of the mold with drained pineapple slices, then add a cherry to the center of each slice. Finely chop the remaining pineapple and set aside. Add the light corn syrup and rum to the bottom of the mold.

Make the sponge cake. Put all the ingredients into a mixing bowl and beat with an electric stand mixer until smooth. Stir in the chopped pineapple, then spoon the mixture into the pineapple-lined mold. Level off the surface usng a metal spatula. Cover the mold with a dome of buttered foil, then stand it in the slow-cooker pot. Pour boiling water into the pot around the mold so that it reaches halfway up the sides of the mold. Cover and cook on high for 4 to 4½ hours or until the sponge cake is well risen, dry to the touch, and a skewer comes out clean when inserted into the center.

Lift the mold out of the slow cooker with oven mitts. Remove the foil, loosen the edge of the sponge cake, then invert onto a plate. Peel off the paper. Serve scoops of the cake in bowls drizzled with hot custard, if liked.

For pineapple & orange upside-down cake, finely grate 1 large orange and squeeze the juice. Add 2 tablespoons of the juice to the mold instead of the rum, then add the grated zest and 1 more tablespoon of the juice to the sponge cake. Cook as above.

marbled chocolate & banana loaf

Preparation time **20 minutes**
Cooking temperature **high**
Cooking time **3 to 3½ hours**
Serves **6**

1 tablespoon **unsweetened cocoa powder**
½ teaspoon **ground cinnamon**
4 teaspoons **boiling water**
½ cup **soft margarine**
½ cup **superfine sugar**
1 cup **all-purpose flour** sifted with 1 teaspoon **baking powder**
2 **eggs**
½ teaspoon **vanilla extract**
1 small **banana**, peeled and mashed
1 **Milky Way bar**, sliced, to decorate

Chocolate sauce
2 **Milky Way bars**, chopped
¼ cup **milk**

Preheat the slow cooker if necessary; see the manufacturer's instructions. Lightly grease a 1 lb loaf pan (first check if it will fit into your slow-cooker pot and, if not, use a solid, round cake pan that will fit) and line the bottom with nonstick parchment paper.

Mix the cocoa, cinnamon, and boiling water together in a bowl until smooth, then let cool. Put the margarine into a bowl or food processor, add the sugar, flour, eggs, and vanilla and beat together well. Spoon half the sponge cake batter into a separate bowl, then beat in the cocoa mixture until smooth. Stir the banana into the cake batter that has not been flavored with cocoa and cinnamon.

Add alternate spoonfuls of cocoa and banana batter to the prepared loaf pan, then run a small knife through the mixtures to marble the batter colors. Cover the pan with a greased dome of foil, then put it into the slow-cooker pot. Pour boiling water into the pot around the pan so that it reaches halfway up the sides. Cover with the lid and cook on high for 3 to 3½ hours or until the top of the sponge cake is dry, well risen, and a skewer comes out clean when inserted into the center. Take the pan out of the slow cooker using oven mitts.

Warm the chopped Milky Way bars and milk in a saucepan, stirring, until smooth. Strain, if needed. Loosen the sides of the cake and turn it out. Decorate with the sliced Milky bar. Cut the loaf into thick slices, serve with the sauce, and vanilla ice cream, if liked.

For marbled chocolate & orange loaf, make the recipe as above, omitting the mashed banana and replacing it with the grated zest of 1 orange.

tutti-frutti spotted dick

Preparation time **20 minutes**
Cooking temperature **high**
Cooking time **2½ to 3½ hours**
Serves **6**

oil or **butter**, for greasing
3 tablespoons **apricot jam**
2 cups **all-purpose flour**
  sifted with 2 teaspoons
  baking powder
½ cup **vegetable shortening**
¼ cup **superfine sugar**
grated zest of 1 **orange**
grated zest of 1 **lemon**
¼ cup **dried cranberries**
½ cup **golden raisins**
½ cup diced **ready-to-eat**
  dried apricots
1 **egg**, beaten
1 cup **skim milk**

Preheat the slow cooker if necessary; see the manufacturer's instructions. Grease a 1 ¼ quart steamed pudding mold with a little oil or butter, then line the bottom with nonstick parchment paper. Spoon the jam into the bottom of the prepared mold.

Put the sifted flour mixture, shortening, sugar, and grated citrus zests into a mixing bowl, then add the dried fruits and stir together. Pour in the egg, then mix in enough milk to make it a soft, spoonable mixture. Spoon the mixture into the jam-lined mold and level off the surface using a metal spatula. Cover with oiled or buttered foil in a slight dome shape so there is room for the pudding to rise.

Put the basin into the slow-cooker pot, then pour enough boiling water into the pot around the mold for it to reach halfway up the sides of the mold. Cover with the lid and cook on high for 2½ to 3½ hours until the pudding is light and fluffy.

Lift the pudding mold out of the slow-cooker pot with oven mitts and remove the foil. Loosen the edge of the pudding with a knife and invert it onto a plate. Scoop it into bowls and serve with hot vanilla custard, if liked.

For coconut & apricot spotted Dick, mix the dry ingredients and citrus zests together. Omit the dried cranberries and golden raisins and add ½ cup desiccated coconut, ¼ cup finely chopped candied citrus peel, and ¾ cup diced ready-to-eat dried apricots instead. Continue as above.

mini blackberry puddings

Preparation time **30 minutes**
Cooking temperature **high**
Cooking time **3½ to 4 hours**
Serves **4**

butter, for greasing
2 cups **all-purpose flour**,
  sifted with 2 teaspoons
  baking powder, plus extra
  flour for dusting
½ cup **vegetable shortening**
½ cup **superfine sugar**,
  divided
grated zest of 1 **lemon**
½ cup **cold water**
1¼ cups **blackberries**
2 large **red plums**, halved,
  pitted, and diced
few drops of **vanilla extract**

Preheat the slow cooker if necessary; see the manufacturer's instructions. Grease 4 x 8 fl oz metal pudding molds (check first that they will fit together in the slow-cooker pot). Put the flour mixture, shortening, half the sugar, and the lemon zest in a mixing bowl. Mix in enough of the water to create a soft but not sticky dough.

Divide the dough into 4 equal portions, then roll out the first piece into a 6-inch disk on a lightly floured surface. Cut out a one-quarter wedge and reserve this for the top. Lift the remaining dough circle into one of the molds, press it gently in, but allowing it to protrude a little above the mold. Press the cut edges together to seal. Repeat with the remaining 3 portions of dough. Fill the molds with the fruit, remaining sugar, and a little vanilla.

Pat each reserved piece of dough into a disk, then roll it out until it is large enough to cover the top of a mold. Stick it in place with a little water, then trim off any excess. Pierce the center of each lid, then cover each mold with a dome of buttered foil. Set the molds in the slow-cooker pot and pour enough boiling water into the pot to reach halfway up the sides of the molds. Cover and cook on high for 3½ to 4 hours until the pastry is light and fluffy. Lift the molds out of the slow cooker using oven mitts, then remove the foil and loosen the edges with a round-bladed knife. Invert each into a shallow bowl and serve drizzled with hot custard, if liked.

For mini apricot puddings, make the pastry and line the molds as above. Fill with the remaining sugar and 2½ cups pitted and diced fresh apricots mixed with 1 tablespoon chopped stem ginger in syrup, adding 1 tablespoon of the ginger syrup. Continue as above.

blackberry & apple eton mess

Preparation time **20 minutes**, plus chilling
Cooking temperature **high**
Cooking time **2½ to 3½ hours**
Serves **6**

1 ¼ lb **apples**, peeled, cored, and chopped
1 cup **blackberries**
½ cup **superfine sugar**
3 tablespoons **water**

To serve
1 ¼ cups **heavy cream**
½ cup **plain yogurt**
2 tablespoons **lemon curd**
3 **ready-made single-serving meringue nests**

Preheat the slow cooker if necessary; see the manufacturer's instructions. Add the apple and blackberries to the slow-cooker pot, sprinkle with the sugar, then add the measurement water. Cover with the lid and cook on high for 2½ to 3½ hours until the fruit has softened. Stir well, then remove the pot from the slow cooker and let cool.

Whip the cream lightly about 30 minutes before serving, then fold in the yogurt and lemon curd. Crumble the meringues into pieces and fold about three-quarters of the meringue pieces into the cream.

Spoon the fruit compote and cream mixture alternately into 6 glass dessert dishes, then run a teaspoon through them to marble the mixtures together. Scatter the tops with the remaining meringue pieces and chill for up to 30 minutes until ready to serve (any longer and the meringue will begin to dissolve).

For peach & raspberry Eton mess, add 1 ¼ lb stoned and diced peaches to the slow-cooker pot with ¼ cup superfine sugar and the juice of 1 lemon. Cover and cook on high for 1 ½ to 2 hours until softened. Stir in 2 cups raspberries, re-cover, and cook for 15 minutes, then let cool. Layer with the cream mixture and meringues as above.

baked honey & orange custards

Preparation time **15 minutes**,
   plus chilling
Cooking temperature **low**
Cooking time **4 to 5 hours**
Serves **4**

2 **eggs**
2 **egg yolks**
1¾ cups **skim milk**
3 teaspoons **superfine sugar**
3 teaspoons **runny honey**
½ teaspoon **vanilla extract**
finely grated zest of ½ **orange**
large pinch of **ground
   cinnamon**

Preheat the slow cooker if necessary; see the manufacturer's instructions. Place the eggs, egg yolks, and milk in a mixing bowl with the sugar, honey, and vanilla and beat until smooth. Strain the mixture through a sieve into a large pitcher, then beat in the orange zest.

Divide the mixture equally between 4 x ½ cup baking dishes or ramekins (checking first that they will all fit together in your slow-cooker pot). Set the dishes in the slow-cooker pot and sprinkle each one with the cinnamon. Pour hot water into the slow-cooker pot around the dishes until it reaches halfway up the sides of the dishes. Cover the tops of the dishes with domed foil, cover with the lid, and cook on low for 4 to 5 hours until set.

Remove the dishes from the slow cooker and let cool. Transfer to the refrigerator to chill well for 3 to 4 hours before serving.

For vanilla crème brûlée, follow the recipe above to cook and chill the custards, using 1 teaspoon vanilla extract and omitting the orange zest and cinnamon. Just before serving, sprinkle 1 teaspoon superfine sugar evenly over the top of each dish and caramelize the sugar with a chef's torch or under a preheated hot broiler. Cool for a few minutes to allow the sugar to set hard, then serve with a few fresh raspberries.

chocolate crème caramels

Preparation time **25 minutes**,
  plus chilling
Cooking temperature **low**
Cooking time **3 to 4 hours**
Serves **4**

2 tablespoons **unsweetened
  cocoa powder**
2 teaspoons **instant coffee**
2 tablespoons **boiling water**
2 **eggs**
2 **egg yolks**
2 tablespoons **superfine
  sugar**
2 cups **skim milk**

Caramel
½ cup **granulated sugar**
5 tablespoons **cold water**
2 tablespoons **boiling water**

Preheat the slow cooker if necessary. For the caramel,
place the sugar in a heavy saucepan with the cold water.
Cook over low heat, without stirring, until the sugar has
completely dissolved. Increase the heat and boil for
5 to 8 minutes or until rich golden brown.

Remove the pan from the heat and add the boiling water,
but be careful because the syrup can spit. Keeping the
pan at arm's length, tilt it around to mix, then divide the
syrup among 4 x 7 fl oz metal pudding molds. Swirl the
caramel around the bottom and up the insides of each
mold. Let stand to cool for 10 minutes.

Put the cocoa, coffee, and boiling water into a mixing
bowl and stir to create a smooth paste. Add the eggs,
egg yolks, and sugar and stir until smooth.

Pour the milk into the empty caramel pan and bring just
to a boil. Gradually whisk the hot milk into the cocoa
mixture, then strain through a sieve into a pitcher. Divide
the mixture among the caramel-lined molds, cover the
tops with greased foil, and put the molds into the slow-
cooker pot. Pour enough boiling water into the slow-
cooker pot to come halfway up the sides of the molds,
then cover with the lid and cook on low for 3 to 4 hours
until set. Remove from the slow cooker and let cool, then
chill in the refrigerator for 3 to 4 hours or overnight.

To serve, dip the molds in hot water, count to 10, then
loosen the edges with a round-bladed knife and invert
each one onto a shallow dish to serve.

For vanilla crème caramels, follow the caramel recipe
above and use it to line the molds. Mix 2 eggs with 3 egg
yolks, 2 tablespoons superfine sugar, and 1 teaspoon
vanilla extract. Add the hot milk and continue as above.

added
extras

duck, pork & apple rillettes

Preparation time **30 minutes**,
  plus chilling
Cooking temperature **high**
Cooking time **5 to 6 hours**
Serves **4**

2 **duck legs**
1 lb **rindless strips of pork belly**, halved
1 **onion**, cut into wedges
1 **Granny Smith apple**, peeled, cored, and thickly sliced
2 to 3 **thyme sprigs**
1 cup **chicken stock**
½ cup **hard cider** or **extra chicken stock**, if preferred
salt and **pepper**

Preheat the slow cooker if necessary; see the manufacturer's instructions. Put the duck legs and pork belly pork strips into the bottom of the slow-cooker pot. Tuck the onion and apple between the pieces of meat and add the thyme sprigs.

Pour the stock and cider, if using, into a saucepan and add plenty of salt and pepper. Bring to a boil, then pour the mixture into the slow-cooker pot. Cover with the lid and cook on high for 5 to 6 hours or until the duck and pork are cooked through and tender.

Lift the meat out of the slow-cooker pot with a slotted spoon and transfer to a large plate, then let cool for 30 minutes. Peel off the duck skin and remove the bones. Shred the duck and pork into small pieces and discard the thyme sprigs. Scoop out the apple and onion with a slotted spoon, finely chop, and mix with the meat. Then taste and adjust the seasoning if necessary.

Pack the meat mixture into 4 individual dishes or small wide-mouth canning jars and press down firmly. Spoon the juices from the slow-cooker pot evenly over the meat to cover and seal it. Let cool, then transfer to the refrigerator and chill well. When the fat has solidified on the top, cover each dish with a lid or plastic wrap and store, chilled, for up to 5 days. Serve the rillettes with warm crusty bread and a few radishes, if liked.

For chicken, pork & prune rillettes, omit the duck and put 2 chicken legs into the slow-cooker pot with the pork belly, onion, and thyme, replacing the apple with ¼ cup ready-to-eat pitted prunes. Continue as above.

fish terrine

Preparation time **30 minutes**,
   plus cooling
Cooking temperature **high**
Cooking time **3 to 4 hours**
Serves **6 to 8**

oil, for greasing
12 oz **boneless cod**, or other
   white fish, cubed
2 **egg whites**
grated zest of ½ **lemon**
juice of 1 **lemon**, divided
1 cup **heavy cream**
4 oz **smoked salmon** or **trout**,
   sliced, divided
5 oz **salmon** or **trout fillet**,
   thinly sliced
salt and **pepper**

Preheat the slow cooker if necessary; see the manufacturer's instructions. Lightly oil a soufflé dish with a capacity of 1 quart and line the bottom with nonstick parchment paper (check first that the dish will fit in the slow-cooker pot). Blend the cod, egg whites, lemon zest, half the lemon juice, and salt and pepper in a food processor until coarsely chopped, then slowly add the cream. Blend until just starting to thicken.

Arrange half the smoked fish slices in the bottom of the dish. Spoon in half the fish mousse and level off the surface. Mix the fish fillet slices with the remaining lemon juice and some pepper, then arrange them on top. Add the remaining mousse and set the remaining smoked fish on top.

Cover the top of the dish with foil. Lower the dish into the slow-cooker pot, then pour enough boiling water into the pot around the dish to come halfway up the sides of the dish. Cover and cook on high for 3 to 4 hours or until the fish is cooked through and the terrine is set.

Lift the dish out of the slow-cooker pot using oven mitts. Let cool for 2 hours. Loosen the edge, invert the terrine onto a plate, and peel off the lining paper. Cut into thick slices. Serve with salad and toast, if liked.

For smoked haddock & chive terrine, make the mousse as above and flavor it with ¼ cup snipped chives, 2 tablespoons chopped capers, and the grated zest and juice of ½ a lemon. Omit the smoked fish. Arrange 1 sliced tomato on the bottom of the dish. Cover with half the fish mousse, 5 oz thinly sliced smoked cod, then the remaining fish mousse. Continue as above.

potted pork with mustard

Preparation time **20 minutes,**
   plus cooling
Cooking temperature **high**
Cooking time **5 to 6 hours**
Serves **4**

1 ¼ lb **pork belly slices**
1 **onion**, chopped
3 **thyme sprigs**, plus extra
   leaves to garnish
½ cup **boiling chicken stock**
2 teaspoons **wholegrain
   mustard**
¼ cup **cream sherry** or **extra
   chicken stock**, if preferred
salt and **pepper**

Preheat the slow cooker if necessary; see the
manufacturer's instructions. Arrange the pork snugly
in a tight-fitting layer in the bottom of the slow-cooker
pot. Scatter with the onion and add the thyme sprigs.

Mix the boiling stock with the mustard, sherry, if using,
and a little salt and pepper. Pour the mixture evenly over
the pork. Cover with the lid and cook on high for 5 to 6
hours until the pork is very tender.

Discard the thyme sprigs, then transfer each pork slice,
1 at a time to a plate, discard the skin and fat, and put
the meat onto another plate. Continue until all the meat
is on one plate and the trimmings are on the other.
Shred the meat into small pieces with a knife and fork.

Strain the juices from the slow-cooker pot. Pack the
pork and a little of the onion into 2 wide-mouth canning
jars, moistening them with a little of the strained
cooking liquid. Press the pork down firmly, then spoon
the remaining cooking liquid all over the meat to cover it
completely. Scatter it with a few extra thyme leaves. Let
cool, then seal the lids and store in the refrigerator for
up to 5 days. To serve, remove the top layer of fat from
the jars and scoop the potted pork onto warm crusty
bread, if liked.

For potted pork with peppercorns, omit the
wholegrain mustard and add 1 teaspoon Dijon mustard.
Cook as above, then shred the pork and finely chop
the prunes. Mix with 1 teaspoon coarsely crushed
peppercorns and 1 teaspoon drained and chopped
capers, then pack into a jar with some of the strained
juices and a little onion as above.

garlicky pork terrine

Preparation time **30 minutes**,
   plus overnight chilling
Cooking temperature **high**
Cooking time **5 to 6 hours**
Serves **6 to 8**

12 **strips smoked bacon**,
   about ½ lb in total
½ lb **ground pork**
½ lb **turkey or chicken breast
   strips**, chopped
5 oz **chicken livers**, defrosted
   if frozen, any white cores
   discarded, then finely
   chopped
2 **scallions**, finely chopped
2 **garlic cloves**, minced
3 tablespoons **brandy**
½ cup **fresh bread crumbs**
1 **egg**, beaten
¼ teaspoon **ground cloves**
1 teaspoon coarsely crushed
   black peppercorns
6 oz chilled ready-made
   chimichurri or 1 cup
   **marinated pimento-stuffed
   green olives**, halved
salt

Preheat the slow cooker, if necessary; see the manufacturer's instructions. Line the bottom of a soufflé dish with a diameter of 6 inches and 3¼ inches high with nonstick parchment paper. Stretch a few of the strips of bacon with the back of a knife to 1½ times as long. Use to line the bottom and sides of the dish, reserving a few to cover the top. Chop the remaining bacon and add it to a large mixing bowl with the pork, turkey or chicken, livers, scallions, and garlic. Mix in the brandy, if using, bread crumbs, egg, and cloves, then season. Sprinkle the chimichurri sauce or olives onto the mixture, then gently fold together. Spoon the mixture into the bacon-lined dish and press down well. Fold the edges of the bacon over the top, then cover with the remaining stretched-out bacon slices, trimming to fit.

Cover the dish with nonstick parchment paper and foil and put it into the slow-cooker pot. Pour enough boiling water into the pot to reach halfway up the sides of the dish, then cover and cook on high for 5 to 6 hours until cooked through (the blade of a small knife inserted into the center of the terrine and held for 10 seconds should feel hot when removed and any juices should run clear).

Remove the dish from the slow cooker with oven mitts, set it on a plate, and cover the top with a plate to act as a weight. Chill overnight. To serve, uncover, run a knife around the dish, invert the dish onto a plate, then, holding the dish and plate, jerk to release. Peel off the paper and scrape off any excess jelly. Cut into slices to serve.

For garlicky pork & pimento terrine, omit the olives and add 1 cup drained red pimento from a jar, cut into small pieces. Continue as above.

best-ever barbecue sauce

Preparation time **15 minutes**
Cooking temperature **high**
Cooking time **5 to 6 hours**
Makes **about 2 lb**

2 **onions**, finely chopped
2 **apples**, weighing 14½ oz
  in total, peeled, cored, and
  finely chopped
2 cups **tomato puree**
¼ cup **dark brown sugar**
2 tablespoons **sherry vinegar**
1 tablespoon **Worcestershire
  sauce**
1 teaspoon **dry English
  mustard powder**
salt and **pepper**

Preheat the slow cooker if necessary; see the manufacturer's instructions. Add all the ingredients to the slow-cooker pot. Stir together, then cover with the lid and cook on high for 5 to 6 hours, stirring once during cooking and again at the end.

Pour into warm, dry jars to the very top, then seal the lids. Label and let cool. Store in the refrigerator for up to 1 month or pack into plastic containers and freeze for up to 3 months. Defrost in the refrigerator overnight. Serve with burgers, sausages, or steak, if liked.

For Cajun sauce, add 1 teaspoon ground allspice, 1 teaspoon ground cinnamon, ½ teaspoon hot smoked paprika, and 1 teaspoon crushed red chile flakes to the other barbecue sauce ingredients. Cook as above.

christmas cranberry sauce

Preparation time **10 minutes**
Cooking temperature **high**
Cooking time **3 to 4 hours**
Serves **10**

1 lb **fresh cranberries**
½ cup **superfine sugar**
½ cup **ruby port** or **fresh orange juice**
juice of **1 orange**
2 teaspoons **cornstarch** (optional)

Preheat the slow cooker if necessary; see the manufacturer's instructions. Add the cranberries to the slow-cooker pot, sprinkle with the sugar, then pour in the port, if using, and orange juice.

Cover and cook on high for 3 to 4 hours until the cranberries are softened. Stir well, coarsely crushing any large berries. If you prefer a slightly thicker sauce, mix the cornstarch to a smooth paste with 1 tablespoon cold water, then stir the paste into the hot sauce, re-cover, and cook for 10 minutes. Spoon into a wide-mouth canning jar, let cool, then seal it with the lid. Store in the refrigerator for up to 1 week.

For cranberry sauce with ginger, omit the port and add ½ cup ginger wine and a 1-inch piece of peeled and finely chopped fresh ginger root.

fiery tropical chutney

Preparation time **25 minutes**
Cooking temperature **high**
Cooking time **4 to 5 hours**
Makes **4 x 12 oz jars**

1 cup **distilled malt vinegar**
1¼ cups **granulated sugar**
2 large **red chiles**, halved,
   seeded, and finely chopped
1½-inch piece of **fresh ginger
   root**, peeled and finely
   chopped
2 teaspoons **black mustard
   seeds**
1 teaspoon **cumin seeds**,
   coarsely crushed
1 teaspoon **coriander seeds**,
   coarsely crushed
½ teaspoon **turmeric**
½ teaspoon **salt**
pepper
2 large **mangoes**, peeled,
   seeded, and diced
1 large **pineapple**, peeled,
   cored, and diced
2 **onions**, finely chopped

Preheat the slow cooker if necessary; see the manufacturer's instructions. Put the vinegar and sugar in a saucepan and heat gently, stirring, until the sugar has dissolved. Mix in the red chiles, ginger, seeds, turmeric, salt, and pepper.

Put the mangoes, pineapple, and onions into the slow-cooker pot, pour in the hot vinegar mixture, then cover and cook on high for 4 to 5 hours until the fruit is almost translucent.

Mash the fruit slightly, if liked, then ladle the chutney into warm, dry jars to the very top, making sure there are no air pockets. Seal with screw-top lids, label, and let cool. Store in a cool, dry place for up to 3 months. Once opened, store in the refrigerator and consume within 2 weeks.

For sweet tropical mango & pineapple chutney, omit the chiles and continue as above.

spicy tomato "sandwich" chutney

Preparation time **20 minutes**
Cooking temperature **high**
Cooking time **6 to 7 hours**
Makes **5 x 12 oz jars**

1 lb **apples**, peeled, cored,
and diced
1 lb **butternut squash**,
peeled, seeded, and diced
1 lb **onions**, finely chopped
1 lb **tomatoes**, coarsely
chopped (no need to remove
skins, unless preferred)
¾ cup packed **golden raisins**
1 teaspoon **crushed red
chile flakes**
1 teaspoon **ground ginger**
1 teaspoon **turmeric**
1 teaspoon **cumin seeds**,
coarsely crushed
1 teaspoon **salt**
1 cup packed **light brown
sugar**
1 cup **red wine vinegar**

Preheat the slow cooker if necessary; see the
manufacturer's instructions. Add the apples, vegetables,
and golden raisins to the slow-cooker pot. Sprinkle with
the spices, salt, and sugar and stir together.

Pour in the vinegar, cover with the lid, and cook on high
for 6 to 7 hours, stirring the chutney once and again
at the end, until the vegetables are soft. If you prefer
a fine-textured chutney, mash the cooked chutney.

Spoon the hot chutney into warm, dry jars to the
very top and press down well, ensuring there are no
air pockets. Seal with a screwtop lid, then store in a
cool, dry place for up to 3 months. Let the chutney
stand for at least 2 to 3 days before serving so that the
flavors can mellow. Once opened, store in the refrigerator
and consume within 2 weeks. Add to cheese or ham
sandwiches or try in hot toasted sandwiches, if liked.

For spicy tomato & zucchini chutney, omit the
butternut squash and replace with 3 cups diced zucchini
and 1 red bell pepper, cored, seeded, and diced.
Continue as above.

old-fashioned lemon & lime curd

Preparation time **20 minutes**
Cooking temperature **low**
Cooking time **3 to 4 hours**
Makes **2 x 12 oz jars**

1 stick **unsalted butter**
2 cups **superfine sugar**
grated zest and juice of
  2 **lemons**
grated zest and juice of
  3 **limes**
4 **eggs**, beaten

Preheat the slow cooker if necessary; see the manufacturer's instructions. Put the butter and sugar into a saucepan, add the citrus zests, then strain in the citrus juices. Heat gently for 2 to 3 minutes, stirring occasionally, until the butter has melted and the sugar has dissolved.

Pour the mixture into a bowl that will fit comfortably into the slow-cooker pot. Let cool for 10 minutes, then gradually strain in the beaten eggs and mix well.

Cover the bowl with foil and place it in the slow-cooker pot. Pour boiling water into the slow-cooker pot around the bowl so that it reaches halfway up the sides of the bowl, then cover with the lid and cook on low for 3 to 4 hours, stirring once, until the curd is thick and falls slowly from a spoon.

Take the bowl out of the slow cooker using oven mitts, stir once more, then spoon it into 2 warm, dry jars. Add a wax-paper disk to the top of each jar, then screw on the lid to seal. Let cool, then store in the refrigerator for up to 3 weeks.

For orange & cranberry curd, add the butter and sugar to a saucepan. Add the grated zest of 1 orange and 2 lemons, then strain in the juice. Add the eggs, then mix in ½ cup finely chopped dried cranberries and cook as above.

clementine marmalade

Preparation time **30 minutes**
Cooking temperature **high**
Cooking time **4 to 5 hours**
Make **6 x 12 oz jars**

2 lb **clementines**, washed
    and quartered
1 quart **boiling water**
juice of 2 **lemons**
4 lb **sugar**

Preheat the slow cooker if necessary; see the manufacturer's instructions. Finely chop the clementines in batches in a food processor or using a knife. Add the chopped fruit and any juices to the slow-cooker pot.

Pour the boiling water evenly over the clementines, cover with the lid, and cook on high for 4 to 5 hours or until the fruit zests are very soft.

Transfer the mixture to a large saucepan, add the lemon juice and sugar, and heat gently, stirring from time to time, until the sugar has completely dissolved.

Bring the marmalade to a boil and boil rapidly for 15 to 20 minutes until a set is reached. To test, spoon a little marmalade onto a cold saucer, let stand for 1 to 2 minutes, then run your finger through the marmalade. If the marmalade has set it should wrinkle and leave a trail where your fingertip has been.

Ladle the marmalade into warm, dry jars right to the top. Screw on the lids, label, and let cool. Store in a cool place for up to 3 months and store in the refrigerator once opened. Consume within 2 weeks.

For orange & lemon marmalade, finely chop 4 oranges and 3 lemons in place of the clementines and cook as above. Tie the seeds from the fruit in a square of cheesecloth and add to the slow cooker and later the saucepan when cooking. Stir in the sugar, omitting the lemon juice, and boil to setting point. Discard the bag of seeds just before spooning into jars. Jar and store as above.

skier's hot chocolate

Preparation time **10 minutes**
Cooking temperature **low**
Cooking time **2 to 3 hours**
Serves **4**

3½ oz good-quality
  semisweet chocolate,
  broken into pieces
2 tablespoons **superfine**
  sugar
3¼ cups **whole milk**
few drops of **vanilla extract**
¼ teaspoon **ground**
  cinnamon
3 tablespoons **Kahlúa coffee**
  liqueur (optional)
mini marshmallows, to serve

Preheat the slow cooker if necessary; see the manufacturer's instructions. Put the chocolate and sugar in the slow-cooker pot, then add the milk, vanilla extract, and cinnamon.

Cover with the lid and cook on low for 2 to 3 hours, whisking once or twice, until the chocolate has melted and the drink is hot. Stir in the Kahlúa, if using. Ladle into mugs and top with a few mini marshmallows.

For hot chocolate with brandy cream, make the hot chocolate as above, replacing the Kahlúa with 3 tablespoons brandy, if using. Whip ½ cup heavy cream with 2 tablespoons powdered sugar until soft peaks form, then gradually whisk in 3 tablespoons brandy, if liked. Pour the hot chocolate into mugs, then top with spoonfuls of the whipped cream and dust lightly with cocoa or finely grated chocolate.

hot mexican coffee

Preparation time **10 minutes**
Cooking temperature **low**
Cooking time **2 to 3 hours**
Serves **4**

½ cup **unsweetened
    cocoa powder**
4 teaspoons **instant
    coffee granules**
1 quart **boiling water**
½ cup **dark rum** (optional)
½ cup **superfine sugar**
½ teaspoon **ground
    cinnamon**
1 large **dried** or **fresh red
    chile** halved, plus extra
    to decorate (optional)
½ cup **heavy cream**
2 tablespoons grated
    semisweet chocolate,
    to decorate

Preheat the slow cooker if necessary; see the manufacturer's instructions. Put the unsweetened cocoa powder and instant coffee in a bowl and mix to a smooth paste with a little of the boiling water.

Pour the cocoa paste into the slow-cooker pot. Add the remaining boiling water, the rum, if using, sugar, cinnamon, and red chile and mix together. Cover with the lid and cook on low for 2 to 3 hours until piping hot or until the coffee is required.

Stir well, discard the chile, then ladle into heatproof glasses. Whip the cream until it is just beginning to hold its shape and spoon a little into each glass. Decorate each drink with a little grated chocolate and a dried chile, if liked.

For hot mocha coffee, reduce the amount of boiling water to 3¾ cups and use 1 teaspoon vanilla extract instead of the rum and chile. Cook as above, then whisk in 1¼ cups milk. Pour into heatproof glasses, top with whipped cream as above. Decorate with a few mini marshmallows, if liked.

campfire mulled cider

Preparation time **5 minutes**
Cooking temperature **high**
  and **low**
Cooking time **3 to 4 hours**
Serves **6**

1 quart **hard, dry cider**
½ cup **whisky**
1 **vanilla bean**, slit
1½-inch piece of **fresh
  ginger root**, peeled and
  thinly sliced
1 **cinnamon stick**, broken in 2
1 cup packed **light brown
  sugar**
½ stick **butter**

Preheat the slow cooker if necessary; see manufacturer's instructions. Pour the cider and whisky into the slow-cooker pot. Scrape the seeds from the vanilla bean, then add these and the bean to the slow-cooker pot along with the ginger, cinnamon, and sugar.

Cover with the lid and cook on high for 1 hour. Reduce the heat and cook on low for 2 to 3 hours until piping hot. Add the butter, stir until melted, then ladle into heatproof glasses, discarding the vanilla bean.

For honeyed cinnamon mulled cider, omit the vanilla and sugar and add to the slow-cooker pot ¼ cup runny honey and the zest from 1 orange, pared off in strips, along with the squeezed juice. Continue as above.

blackberry mulled wine

Preparation time **5 minutes**
Cooking temperature **high**
   and **low**
Cooking time **3 to 4 hours**
Serves **6**

1 bottle of **red wine**
½ cup **dark rum**
1 cup **orange juice**
1¾ cups **cold water**
¾ cup **superfine sugar**
1¼ cups **blackberries**
1 **cinnamon stick**, broken into
   2 pieces
1 **orange**, halved and sliced,
   to serve

Preheat the slow cooker if necessary; see the manufacturer's instructions. Pour the wine, rum, orange juice, and measurement water into the slow-cooker pot. Add the sugar, blackberries, and cinnamon and stir together.

Cover with the lid and cook on high for 1 hour, then reduce the heat to low and continue to cook for 2 to 3 hours. Ladle into heatproof glasses and serve each with a half slice of orange.

For traditional mulled wine, omit the blackberries and heat the red wine, orange juice, and water with sugar and 2 cinnamon sticks, adding 1 orange, cut into chunks and spiked with 4 cloves, plus a little grated nutmeg and a 1-inch piece of fresh ginger root, peeled and thinly sliced. Cook as above.

index

236

acknowledgments

Executive Editor Eleanor Maxfield
Senior Editor Leanne Bryan
Designer Jaz Bahra
Design and Art Direction Penny Stock
Photographer William Shaw
Home Economist Sara Lewis
Props Stylist Kim Sullivan
Production Controller Allison Gonsalves

Photography by William Shaw/Octopus Publishing Group

Additional photography:
Octopus Publishing Group Stephen Conroy 11, 27, 33, 37, 41, 63, 73, 89, 95, 103, 117, 121, 123, 147, 173, 179, 181, 207, 209, 227, 229; William Shaw 57, 91, 127, 149, 153, 201, 203.

Slow cookers kindly loaned for testing and photography from Morphy Richards.